INTERMITTENT FASTING FOR WOMEN

A COMPLETE GUIDE TO FASTING FOR WEIGHT LOSS, BURN FAT AND IMPROVE THE QUALITY OF YOUR LIFE

By Susan Lombardi

Table of Contents

Introduction

Welcome to intermittent fasting for women! Thank you for finding this book worth your time and attention. Herein you'll find comprehensive information on intermittent fasting for women. The book elaborates how this form of fasting can transform your life by ushering you into a healthier lifestyle.

Whether you're hearing about intermittent fasting for the first time or have some information and you want to dig deeper, you will find chapter after chapter of comprehensive guidelines directing you on how to get into the fast and what to expect along the way.

This may be the first step on a long journey, to finally gaining the health, energy, vitality and gorgeous body that you've always dreamed of. The beauty of intermittent fasting is that it's very easy to use and works for most people. There are some folks that probably shouldn't use intermittent fasting and we'll discuss the issues with that in the book. But for most people, intermittent fasting is a great way to lose weight and feel great – as well as look your best.

Intermittent fasting will help you lose weight very rapidly and get your body into much better health than it is now. One of the problems that we have with the standard American diet is that too many people have insulin problems. You may not be diabetic, but you're probably suffering from problems related to insulin and blood sugar just the same.

Intermittent fasting can correct these problems very quickly. As you probably know, high insulin levels and more likely in overweight people.

More overweight you are, greater the amount of fat in your body and so your blood sugar levels also increases.

One of the goals of intermittent fasting is to jumpstart the metabolic system. Or maybe we should say it will reset the metabolic system, curing you of problems like insulin resistance. No matter what style of eating you choose, intermittent fasting can be very beneficial. Even better, intermittent fasting can correct these problems very quickly.

One of the reasons that intermittent fasting is becoming so popular is that it is very flexible. When you hear about fasting, you're probably thinking that it's some kind of hard-core idea that involves going days without eating. But this is it true at all. In fact, many types of intermittent fasting allow you to eat every single day. Some types of intermittent fasting, including the most popular ones, allow you to eat over a large time window during the day which means you can enjoy three square meals and even snacks. So you're hardly going to even notice that you're even fasting at all.

Another benefit of intermittent fasting is that it works with any kind of diet. Just go on YouTube and look for yourself. If you do, you'll see that many people get huge benefits from intermittent fasting without following any kind of diet. Some people are even eating junk food and losing huge amounts of weight. You'll see people eat all kinds of sugar and desserts, but if they do it over a very short time it doesn't affect their body weight or fat composition.

We only mention this to note that it's extremely flexible to use intermittent fasting. So you can go on eating the foods you're eating now,

10

or if you want to maximize your weight loss, you can adopt a low-carb diet. But just keep in mind: you don't need to use a keto diet or any specific to enjoy the benefits of intermittent fasting.

Transformation is the most important word in this book. We will aim to keep transformation as the key goal – not only the transformation of our diet or health but a transformation of our entire lives. If this seems too far out of reach, do not be discouraged – it is easier than you think. Transformation does not require us to change who we truly are. We can keep all the things we love, but it will require a rewiring of how we view ourselves and the world around us. What could normally trigger a negative or detrimental attitude will be altered and viewed from a different perspective, a perspective that comes from a place of self-love and confidence. By applying the knowledge and practices we are about to learn into our lives, we can develop a lifestyle that will become second nature and only help us stay healthful physically and mentally.

In the chapters to come, we will discuss the ins and outs of Intermittent Fasting with an emphasis on women's weight loss in today's busy and complicated world. Women have to battle more difficulties than men for all of written history, and today there's no difference. Naturally, the extra stress on women to look and behave a certain way makes it very difficult to maintain balance during the mundane day-to-day tasks, thus making healthful lifestyles a choice that is overlooked or flat out cannot be obtained.

Chapter 1: What is Intermittent Fasting?

Intermittent Fasting is essentially the practice of restricting mealtimes, reducing snacking, or cutting out days of eating, based on the method one chooses. So many of us snack unconsciously or when we're getting moody without any real hunger. So many of us eat unconsciously in general, and then we're confused why our bodies are holding onto the weight. Intermittent Fasting reminds the body what food is for, and it restarts that nutritional absorption potential. All you have to do is cut out the snacks, fast a few hours a day, or just drink water a few days a week.

Intermittent Fasting (IF) is both a dietary choice and a lifestyle, but those who have the most success with IF will tell you that it became a lifestyle for them almost instantly. Sure, dieting plans and IF can match up nicely, but for some, IF requires no dietary change whatsoever. The point is to eat less and to eat less often. The brain and the body will respond in no time.

Practicing intermittent fasting helps strengthen our bodies to burn fat in contrast with our more common fed state. The body during the fed state relies on frequent resupplies of glucose and sugar for fuel. In addition to weight loss, stimulating and strengthening the metabolism provides numerous other health benefits that include enhanced mental clarity, focus, and stress reduction. The process and practice of intermittent fasting sharpens the mind and neural functions while reshaping the physical structure of our bodies at the cellular and molecular levels.

Whatever timeframe is chosen, the practice of intermittent fasting is possible to incorporate into daily life because it involves fasting that occurs at irregular intervals that are set by the individual and designed according to her preference.

This is the revolutionary secret of intermittent fasting: it can be tailored to the individual woman, rather than requiring her to conform to an extreme or unrealistic regime. This makes it fun and adaptable! You set the rules according to a plan that works for you.

Fasting is a relatively simple practice that yields incredible and complicated results. The effects that fasting has on the body and mind seems unfathomable: weight loss, blood sugar regulation, blood pressure regulation, and growth hormone regulation – only to name a few important ones. In recent years, science has reached full strength to support these claims, not to mention the thousands of online videos of people's results now that fasting has hit the mainstream. There are different types of fasting as well as many ways to fast.

Within the abundant array of different methods and individual changes any one person may implement, there is a wealth of potential ways to impact the health of the body and mind in positive ways. Fasting, in a general and broad definition, is the practice of willingly abstaining from something, usually food and drink. Whether it is simply not eating chocolate for a week or two or even cutting out all solid foods for a month, no matter how large or small the impact the abstinence has on you, that is fasting from your chosen food. Another more intensive fast would be dry fasting. Dry fasting is the complete abstinence from every source of solid or liquid food for any predetermined period, and, of course, willingly. Although not completely out of the question for beginners, these styles of fasting are used more sparingly than the style we aim to focus on, and that practice is called *Intermittent Fasting* or *IF* for short.

Chapter 2: Benefits of Intermittent Fasting

The main benefit of intermittent fasting is weight loss. However, there are several benefits of intermittent fasting, and most of them were widely recognized even in history.

In ancient times, fasting periods and seasons were referred to as cleanses, purifications or detoxifications, but the idea of all of them is the same. That is to do without eating food for a specified period. Ancient people believed that this period of fasting would clear their body systems of any toxin and rejuvenate them.

- Some of the most known benefits of intermittent fasting are:

Improved Mental Concentration and Clarity

Fasting has incredible benefits for the healthy function of the brain. The most known benefit stems from the activation of autophagy, which is a cell cleansing process. Note that fasting has anti-seizure effects.

Since the time immemorial human beings have been known to respond to caloric deprivation with a reduced size of major organs with two exemptions, the male testicles, and the brain.

This preservation of testicle size is a significant benefit because it helps to pass on genes to the next generation. Also, the of cognitive functions is essential for the survival of any human being.

For instance, imagine you are a caveman where food is scarce. When your brain starts to slow down the mental fog will make it harder to get food. Your brain power, one of the major advantages you have in the natural world, could be decreasing. Surviving without food will slowly erode your mental functioning until you are no longer able to perform essential blundering functions, let alone going out to get or to hunt food.

Therefore, for survival, cognitive functions in your body are maintained and boosted during fasting or starvation. This aspect has been known throughout the evolution of humankind. For instance, in ancient Greece, thinkers or scientists used to fast for days.

They fasted not because they wanted to lose some weight. They believed fasting would increase and improve their mental agility. Even today, people marvel at the ancient Greek mathematicians and philosophers. Even in the history of Japanese prisoners during the Second World War people have been describing the unquestionable clarity of thought that accompanies starvation and fasting. This book describes a prisoner who would read several books from his memory and another prisoner who mastered the Norwegian language in a few days.

Healthier Way to Lose Weight

Intermittent fasting is a healthier way for people to lose weight. As a result of the flexibility of this diet, you are still able to continue consuming everything that is healthy for you. Any dietary considerations that you may need to accommodate for can easily be taken into consideration and accounted for with intermittent fasting. This makes it easy and effortless when it comes to losing weight.

Unlike other diets, there are no restricting calories or starving yourself with the intermittent fasting diet. You will not experience any sensations of hunger or feeling as though you are not getting enough. Whereas other diets are often not able to be maintained for long, resulting in unhealthy practices of yo-yo dieting, intermittent fasting can be. This means that the diet is not only healthier but also more sustainable.

When you are eating the intermittent fasting diet, you can look forward to losing fat specifically. This diet supports you in letting go of unwanted tummy fat and other fat on your body that may be stubborn and resistant to other diets. Intermittent fasting is both healthier and more effective in supporting you with reaching your weight loss goals.

Supports Healthy Bodily Functions

Intermittent fasting gives your body time to complete processes and functions before introducing more food into your system. This means that every time you eat, you are giving your body adequate time to actually metabolize the food and use it appropriately. In modern society, we regularly overeat and push our bodies to constantly be in a state of digesting. As a result, our systems become overwhelmed and we do not effectively metabolize everything. This can lead to you not getting enough nutrition, storing fats, and struggling to produce healthy levels of natural hormones and chemicals within your body.

When you eat the intermittent fasting diet, you support your body by giving it enough time to process everything. As a result, its ability to metabolize food and gain everything from it is improved. Your insulin levels drop significantly, which supports your body in burning fat. You also notice an increase in human growth hormone that can reach up to

5x your original value. This supports you in fat burning as well as muscle gain. As a result of your intermittent fasting, your body is able to focus more energy on other processes beyond digesting food. This means that things like cellular repair functions have a greater ability to take place. So, your body has a stronger ability in removing waste materials from your cells and supporting them in healing from any damage that they may experience. Finally, intermittent fasting is known for supporting people with gene expression. This means that this dietary habit can support your genes in changing in ways that actually protect them against diseases and promote a longer lifespan. Your body has a much stronger ability to remain healthy and function optimally when you eat according to the intermittent fasting diet.

Supports You in Healing Faster

When your cells have an easier time restoring themselves and your body is exposed to less stress, you have an easier time in healing faster. This means that any time you place a physical strain on your body, you can look forward to spending less time healing from that experience.

This is beneficial for many reasons. One of the biggest reasons, however, is that when you are able to heal faster you are able to increase your health faster. Activities such as working out and lifting weights require your body to take some downtime to heal in between. Any time you are seeking to increase your muscular strength, you will experience ripping in your muscles. Then, the muscle tissue heals and grows back in a greater quantity. This is what leads to muscle growth. It is also what leads to pain after working out.

When you eat according to the intermittent fasting diet, your ability to heal from this type of damage is improved. This means that you can gain muscle faster and without having a negative impact on your overall health.

In addition to intentional healing that is required after activities such as working out, you will also have an easier time healing from other physical ailments. For example, if you endure an accidental injury your body will have an easier time healing it than it would if you were in ill health. Because your body has an improved ability to repair cells, you can look forward to healing much quicker from any injury that you might experience.

You Can Maintain a More Youthful Appearance

Improved cellular repairs and gene expression is not only great for healing, but it is also great for maintaining a youthful vitality! When these functions improve for you, your body's ability to maintain healthier skin, hair, nails, and other bodily features is improved, too. This means that you can look forward to maintaining a more youthful appearance just by adjusting your diet and eating the intermittent fasting way.

In addition to actually looking more youthful, you can also enjoy the experience of feeling more youthful, too. People who eat the intermittent fasting diet report feeling greater levels of energy. As a result, they are able to start enjoying life with a greater vitality about them. This means that you can enjoy all of the activities that you have been missing as a result of low energy and ill health, like dancing and spending time enjoying life with your loved ones!

Lowers Your Risk of Contracting Diseases

When your immune system is operating optimally and your entire bodily functions are improved, you can enjoy the benefits of lowered risk of contracting diseases. As you already know, diseases like type 2 diabetes, Alzheimer's, and cancer have been prevented by the intermittent fasting diet. However, this diet can also support you in preventing other potential diseases, too.

Eating the intermittent fasting diet has proven to level out blood pressure, reduce bad cholesterol, lower inflammatory markers, and lower blood sugar levels in your blood. This means that you can look forward to having better heart health. You also work toward preventing heart disease by eating this way.

Reduced instances of inflammation markers also mean that the intermittent fasting diet can also support you in preventing or curing symptoms of diseases like fibromyalgia. They can also support you in healing from chronic fatigue syndrome, and other conditions that are typically related to poor inner health.

Your improved diet will also support your healthy brain functions. When you eat in accordance with the intermittent fasting diet, you also support the growth of new nerve cells, as well as a brain-derived neurotrophic factor (BDNF.) Both of these instances can support you in improving brain health and function overall. This means that you are at a lower risk of experiencing clinical depression, or that you may even be able to reverse the symptoms that you have already experienced. Furthermore, this can also support you in recovering from any damage that could be experienced as a result of a stroke.

Reduces Inflammation and Physical Stress

The intermittent fasting diet is known to eliminate free radicals from your body. This means that you are less likely to experience chronic inflammation and physical stress that is based on nutrition and nourishment.

For many people, chronic inflammation and physical stress that is derived from nourishment can be the root cause of many physical symptoms. Often, people go undiagnosed yet continue to experience frustrating symptoms like pain, swelling, headaches, and metabolic issues when they experience chronic inflammation. This can be frustrating and can lead to a feeling of hopelessness and anger when it comes to trying to resume a healthy and active lifestyle. Intermittent fasting may be able to support you in overcoming these symptoms if they are being caused by chronic inflammation or physical stress.

May Extend Your Lifespan

Intermittent fasting has shown in some studies that it may be able to extend your lifespan. Many people find themselves living shorter lives with poorer quality of life as a result of poor health. Disease and illness kill far more people each year than actual old age or natural causes do.

Using the intermittent fasting diet may support you in preventing these illnesses and diseases so that you can live a longer, healthier, natural life.

Although this has not yet been tested in humans, the intermittent fasting diet was tested in lab rats. Through these tests, some studies showed that the rats lived as much as 83% longer than those who did not fast. Despite this specific piece of evidence not yet being tested on humans, there is plenty of evidence that suggests that the factors that prevent longer and healthier lives can be avoided with intermittent fasting. For this reason, we can assume that intermittent fasting may indeed support humans in living longer and healthier lives, too.

Boosts Your Immune System

As a result of the many benefits that you gain from intermittent fasting, you also get to look forward to having an improved immune system. This is from the combination of reduced physical stress, increased cellular reparation abilities, weight loss, and other benefits that you gain from intermittent fasting.

Your boosted immune system will be supportive in preventing you from experiencing long-term health conditions such as various illnesses and diseases. It will also support you in preventing the contraction of less dangerous illnesses such as the common cold and influenza. As a result, you can look forward to spending less time being sick and more time on your feet and enjoying life.

Increased Ketones

Fasting for anywhere from 10-16 hours every single day is said to improve your body's ability to release ketones into your bloodstream. This releasing of ketones encourages your body to consume and burn fat rather than carbohydrates when it comes to producing energy for you throughout the day. This means that using the intermittent fasting diet supports weight loss through actually using your fatty weight as a fuel.

Many people actually choose to combine intermittent fasting with the keto diet as a way to increase weight loss. Furthermore, they find that these two combined eating styles result in them feeling greater energy levels, having healthier bodily functions, and experiencing greater mental clarity. There are many benefits that can be gained from intermittent fasting alone, but when you combine it with the keto diet it can truly be life-changing!

Mental Sharpness and Intermittent Fasting

Consider and think about the large Thanksgiving turkey and pumpkin pie. After that meal, were you mentally sharp? Or were you dull? What about the opposite when you were hungry? Were you slothful and tired? The answer is a big no. When you were hungry, your senses were hyper-alert, and your mind was very sharp. The fact that consuming food would make you concentrate even better is not true. There are survival advantages to human beings that are cognitively sharp. You will also experience physical agility when you are fasting.

When you say that you are hungry for something, such as hungry for attention, hungry for power, does it mean that you are dull and slothful? It does not mean that. It means that your mind is energetic and hyper-vigilant. Hunger and fasting activate you toward your goal. Many people tend to think that fasting would dull their senses, but the truth is that it has an energizing effect.

Therefore, there will be an increase in your brain connectivity and some new neuron growth in your stem cells. This is mediated in part by your brain-derived neurotrophic factor. For women, both fasting and exercise increase brain-derived neurotrophic factor expression in many parts of their brain. BDNF plays a major role in glucose metabolism, appetite, and control of gastrointestinal and cardiovascular systems.

Intermittent Fasting & Neurodegenerative Disorders

There is also another aspect of neurodegenerative diseases and fasting. If you maintain intermittent fasting, you will experience less age-related deterioration of neurons as compared to a person who is on a normal diet. You will also experience fewer symptoms in diseases such as Huntington's, Parkinson's, and Alzheimer's disease.

The benefits of intermittent fasting to your brain can be experienced in both during caloric restriction and fasting. During calorie restriction and exercise, you will experience increased electrical and synaptic activity in your brain.

Intermittent Fasting and Alzheimer's Disorders

These complications are characterized by an abnormal accumulation of proteins in the body cells. There are two classes of Alzheimer's disorders, neurofibrillary tangles and amyloid plaques. The known symptoms of Alzheimer's disorders closely correlate with the accumulation of these tangles and plagues. These abnormal protein accumulations in the body cells are believed to negatively affect the synaptic connections in your memory and the cognition parts of your brain.

Some specific proteins such as HSP-70 are known to prevent damages and misfolding of amyloid and neurofibrillary tangles proteins. Therefore alternate fasting will increase the levels of HSP-70 protein. When amyloid and tau proteins are destroyed beyond repair, they are removed by autophagy. This process is accelerated by Intermittent Fasting.

Intermittent Fasting and Breast Cancer

Low-calorie meals are a strategy to prevent breast cancer. It has beneficial effects on the overall health of breast cells within the breasts of a woman. Overweight women have large fat cells in their breasts, and this increases the amount of estrogen within the breast. They can also store fats in their liver and in their abdomen where it increases the circulation of sex hormones, insulin hormone, inflammation and fat produced hormones. These changes leads to the development of breast cancer.

Intermittent Fasting and Insulin Sensitivity

As far as metabolism of glucose is concerned, intermittent fasting is perfect. It is a powerful tool that normalizes glucose. It also improves the glucose variability.

Chapter 3: Intermittent Fasting Techniques

Now that we have discussed how your body will react to fasting let's discuss the many different forms of fasting. Although there are seemingly infinite ways to go about your Intermittent Fasting routine, we will focus on six methods that are popular among fitness experts and the fasting community. We will discuss the suitable timing of 'eating windows', the duration of time in the day when you are allowed to eat, and compare each method so you can successfully choose the best one for your lifestyle. Although fasting has its roots in religion and spirituality, we will not go extensively into these practices, but if you wish to combine your spiritual goals with these methods, you can go right ahead.

At this point, we would like to state that keeping a fasting notebook helps immensely for someone just starting out. By recording our experiences and documenting how successful or unsuccessful our routine is, we can find insight into ourselves and also organize the aspects of our routine that may need to be altered or customized. It is not mandatory to have a notebook, but throughout this book, we will be keeping track of our experiences and analyzing our regimen to understand better what works for us as individuals.

The 16/8 Method

Also known as the *Leangain's method*, this method was popularized by Martin Berkhan. The eating window for this style is eight hours with a sixteen-hour fasting time. So if you sleep eight hours, awake, then restrict caloric intake for eight hours, then you can eat as much as you like until bedtime. Another example would be to awake, start your eight-hour eating window, then begin fasting for the evening and during sleep. This is a common choice for people who already skip breakfast. Tea and coffee have no calories, so they are still allowed to be consumed, obviously without sugar added.

Overview:

- *Sixteen hours of fasting*

- *Eight-hour consumption window*

- *Zero-calorie drinks allowed*

The 5/2 Diet Method

This method looks more like a diet than a proper fast, but it is a popular method for weight loss and often finds its way into IF circles. First popularized by Michael Mosley, it is also called the 'Fast Diet'.

This method involves your normal eating routine for five days of the week then restricting your caloric intake to 600 calories or less for two days of the week. So you can choose your two days to fast whether they are together or not, let's say Wednesday and Friday.

Then, treat all other days as normal days, but on Wednesday and Friday, you eat one or two small meals that together equal 600 calories or less. This is a great beginner diet to try before you get into some more intensive IF.

If you're wary of how you may react to fasting, then this method is great to start.

Overview:

- *Five days of normal meals according to your daily diet*

- *Two days of consuming 600 calories or less*

The Eat Stop Eat Method

That is 24 hours of no solid food or caloric intake. Unsweetened coffee and tea are acceptable during the fasting days for this method. A great example would be to fast from dinner to dinner or, let's say, from 4:00 pm to 4:00 pm the next day. It does not matter what time frame you choose, but it should be a solid 24-hour period. Keeping to your usual eating schedule on the non-fasting days is important.

Overview:

- *Strict 24-hour fast once or twice a week*

- *Maintain usual eating schedule during non-fast days*

Lean-Gains Method (14:10)

The lean-gains method has several different incarnations on the web, but its fame comes from the fact that it helps shed fat while building it into muscle almost immediately. Through the lean-gains method, you'll find yourself able to shift all that fat to be muscle through a rigorous practice of fasting, eating right, and exercising.

Through this method, you fast anywhere from 14 to 16 hours and then spend the remaining 10 or 8 hours each day engaged in eating and exercise. This method, as opposed to the crescendo, features daily fasting and eating, rather than alternated days of eating versus not. Therefore, you don't have to be quite so cautious about extending the physical effort to exercise on the days you are fasting because those days when you're fasting are literally every day!

For the lean-gains method, start fasting only 14 hours and work it up to 16 if you feel comfortable with it, but never forget to drink enough water and be careful about expending too much energy on exercise! Remember that you want to grow in health and potential through intermittent fasting. You'll certainly not want to lose any of that growth by forcing the process along.

Crescendo Method

This is usually an introduction to fasting, it is how many people begin their fasting journey. This is a less intense form of intermittent fasting and is a great way for you to see how it works to ease your fears and become familiarized with a fasting schedule. This method involves normally for 4 or 5 days a week and then restricting your eating period to between 8 or 10 hours for two or three non-consecutive days. Very similar to the 16/8 method, but instead of doing every day, you only do it a couple days each week. These are the safest ways for women to fast because they do not upset the hormonal balance of the body. Intermittent fasting not done properly can trick the body into going into what is known as starvation mode. This happens when the body thinks it needs to hold onto fat longer because it doesn't know when it will have a chance to consume food for fuel again. This can lead to burning muscle for fuel as well as upsetting the hormonal balance, leading to even more issues. However, intermittent fasting done properly can be safe and incredibly beneficial.

Not only does intermittent fasting help you lose weight, but it also improves mental clarity and allows you to simplify your life in a way that diets do not. Think about how much time you spend worrying about or eating food, and then imagine what other things you could be doing if this were not the case. This is one the major benefits of intermittent fasting, there are no surprises and you are able to take complete control of when you eat.

The Alternating Day Method

This method involves fasting every other day. This method can be customized to your liking on the fast days. You can cut back to 600 calories a day, not unlike the 5/2 method, but fasting every other day. If you feel comfortable, you can intake zero calories on the fast days; this would be a very intense method and is not recommended for beginners. For example, eat normally on Sunday, lower calorie intake to 600 calories or less on Monday, eat normally on Tuesday, lower calorie intake Wednesday, eat normally on Thursday, lower calories on Friday. You see, we hit a snag in our pattern as there is an odd number of days in a week. For the odd day out, in this case, Saturday, you can choose to lower the calorie count or eat regularly. It is up to you. For another example, the

Saturday odd day out, you could potentially fast for 24 hours then jump back into the pattern on Sunday.

Overview:

- *Fast or lower calories every other day*

- *Keep a usual eating schedule on non-fast days*

- *Choose what suits you best for the odd day out*

The Warrior Method

This method was popularized by Ori Hofmekler. It includes eating small amounts of raw plant-based foods during the day, then one large meal during the evening. Essentially, you are fasting all day and breaking the fast at night. This diet typically focuses on eating raw and unprocessed foods to get the full benefit. For example, during the day, you snack on fruits, veggies, and nuts. Once the evening comes, you prepare a large meal that is as unprocessed and raw as possible.

Overview:

- *Light amounts of raw foods or completely fasting during daylight hours*

- *A large meal at night, as unprocessed and raw as possible*

20:4 Method

Stepping things up a notch from the 14:10 and 16:8 methods, the 20:4 method is a tough one to master, for it is rather unforgiving. People talk about this method of intermittent fasting as intense and highly restrictive, but they also say that the effects of living this method are almost unparalleled with all other tactics.

For the 20:4 method, you'll fast for 20 hours each day and squeeze all your meals, all your eating, and all your snacking into 4 hours. People who attempt 20:4 normally have two smaller meals or just one large meal and a few snacks during their 4-hour window to eat, and it really is up to the individual which four hours of the day they devote to eating.

The trick for this method is to make sure you're not overeating or bingeing during those 4-hour windows to eat. It is all-too-easy to get hungry during the 20-hour fast and have that feeling then propel you into intense and unrealistic hunger or meal sizes after the fast period is over. Be careful if you try this method. If you're new to intermittent fasting, work your way up to this one gradually, and if you're working your way up already, only make the shift to 20:4 when you know you're ready. It would surely disappoint if all your progress with intermittent fasting got hijacked by one poorly thought-out goal with 20:4 method.

Meal Skipping

Meal skipping is an extremely flexible form of intermittent fasting that can provide all of the benefits of intermittent fasting but with less of the strict scheduling. If you are not someone who has a typical schedule or who feels as though a more strict variation of the intermittent fasting diet will serve you, meal skipping is a viable alternative.

Many people who choose to use meal skipping find it to be a great way to listen to their body and follow their basic instincts. If they are not hungry, they simply don't eat that meal. Instead, they wait for the next one. Meal skipping can also be helpful for people who have time constraints and who may not always be able to get in a certain meal of the day.

It is important to realize that with meal skipping, you may not always be maintaining a 10-16-hour window of fasting. As a result, you may not get every benefit that comes from other fasting diets. However, this may be a great solution to people who want an intermittent fasting diet that feels more natural to them. It may also be a great idea for those who are looking to begin listening to their body more so that they can adjust to a more intense variation of the diet with greater ease. In other words, it can be a great transitional diet for you if you are not ready to jump into one of the other fasting diets just yet.

The Spontaneity Method

This method is the loosest and most flexible method of IF. The method is pretty straight forward; there are no guidelines or structures. Simply skip a meal when it's convenient or if you're not hungry. Skipping one or two meals every so often can be a great foundation to lay while you search for a more suitable routine. This method also comes in handy for busy people, parents, or just people who love winging it.

Overview:

- *No structure*

- *Simply skip meals when convenient, or fast whenever you like*

Now that we have a general idea of different fasting techniques, keep in mind that these are guidelines that can be customized to fit your specific lifestyle. To reiterate: no one way suits everyone. So as you analyze these methods, keep in mind your personal life and how you alter the structures not only to fit into your schedule but also to personalize your practice. By personalizing your routine, you allow yourself some added empowerment and something that you helped create. Some examples of customizing your practice can include changing the length of fasts, changing diet to suit (vegan, Paleo, etc.), and/or changing the fasting patterns (alternating every two days, etc.). With the methods above, we see many similarities between them. With the main premise being a caloric restriction and eating window restriction, these methods are simply different customized versions of fasting itself. So this means that we can customize these methods to suit our needs and preferences as individuals.

When we decide to customize a method, it needs to be well thought out. Why do I need these customizations? Are these customizations feasible as something I can accomplish? There is an infinite number of ways we can change and alter these techniques, and we will provide some examples below. Keep in mind these are not the only ways to customize but just some basic strategies.

Customize as you please, but be safe and mindful in doing so:

- **Customization Strategy #1**: *Altering the duration of eating windows*

We see above that one of the main differences in these methods is the timing. For example, the 16/8 method requires eating for eight hours of the day and fasting for sixteen hours of the day. This can be altered easily to suit you. Need a little extra time for the eating window? Add an hour. Feeling confident that you can shorten the eating window? Shorten it an hour or two. You can also choose your eating window during the day. Morning, midday or night are all suitable times to eat depending on your schedule.

- **Customization Strategy #2**: *Altering days*

Days in which you choose to fast are very important but not limited to the guidelines above. The alternating method as an example, alternating days of fasting is a simple pattern, but what if you need two days off from fasting? Make your fast days every third day. Another example would be putting more fast days together, as with the Eat Stop Eat method. Instead of one or two days of complete calorie restriction, maybe do three or push your two days back-to-back for a more challenging fast.

- **Customization Strategy #3**: *Altering the timing of meals*

Much content online will suggest a proper time for having your meals or will cite the warrior method as an example that requires a large meal at night. This large meal can be placed anywhere in the day according to your preference; in fact, many people prefer their large meal in the middle of the day to avoid a full stomach while sleeping.

- **Customization strategy #4**: *Altering meal choices*

As noted above, the warrior method requires raw foods to be ingested. Many people have dietary restrictions and preferences that may not fit into these diets and methods, so switch it up! What you eat during your IF routines is important, and you want to keep it healthy. But be reasonable with yourself; choose foods you enjoy. If you prefer fried, greasy foods, maybe try the same ingredients but prepared differently – baked chicken instead of breaded and fried, etc.

- **Customization strategy #5**: *Include your lifestyle*

When we research fasting online, we see a pattern – health blogs with muscular people in their fitness attire smiling brightly in front of a sunset. This is all fine for some people, but many do not relate to this lifestyle. Lucky for us, fasting is for everyone. You can add fasting to your normal routine easily without hitting the gym or buying spandex. Make it a point to meld IF into your lifestyle rather than view it as something separate from you. Any hobby you love – gaming, fishing, reading, music, art, scrapbooking, etc. – can be a part of your fasting routine. In fact, having a low-intensity hobby is great for the downtime during fasts.

Chapter 4: Choosing the right fasting regime

When you make your choice from the different options listed above, there are several things you'll want to keep in mind. First and foremost, amongst those things will be the fact that you can always choose another method (or a more flexible one to start with) in case something doesn't work as you'd hoped. Ultimately, you'll also want to keep the following points in mind as you go about selecting your method: body type & abilities, lifestyle, daily tendencies, work routine, friends & family, and dietary choices. For all these considerations, remember what feels best to you, and remember to keep your goals with IF in mind at all times!

Consider your body type and abilities:

Think of how your body looks and feels and how much about it you'd like to change. Think about how you react to food and what it looks like when you're hungry. Think about those things you view as your "limits" and how comfortable you are with pushing. Are you a fitness freak or a couch potato? Are you huskier or slimmer? Does your body hold onto fat or build muscle quickly? Do you retain water weight or not? Do you work out? Do you require a lot of water when you do? Consider all these things about your body and more, then compare them to the methods listed above.

Consider your lifestyle:

When do you normally wake up and how much sleep do you get on an average night? How hungry are you normally when you do wake up? How fast is your metabolism and when do you notice its peak? How do you make your living? Do you spend a lot of time in the car or on your feet or in an office? Are you constantly around other people or are you often alone? When you choose your method for Intermittent Fasting, make sure to consider all these lifestyle points. Maybe you wouldn't want to choose a method that forces you to eat when you're supposed to be at work.

Consider your daily tendencies:

Do you eat mostly in the daylight hours or after the sun goes down? Do you go to work in the daytime or night time? Are you generally nocturnal, diurnal, or crepuscular? Do you have a lot of freedom and flexibility in your daily routines? Do you travel a lot for work? Do you spend a lot of time on the move? Do you have trouble remembering to eat? Are you the type of person that works out on the regular? Consider these themes in your life and more before you choose your method. Does it make sense for you to have low intake days where you consume 500 calories or less? Or does it make more sense for you to have extended periods in each day where you're just not eating based on your habits or tendencies or otherwise? Plan something that makes sense and respects your habits so that the transition into Intermittent Fasting is as easy and painless as possible.

Consider your work routine:

Do you go to work in the morning or night? Are you allowed to eat at work? Do you work around food or in the food service industry? Do you work on your feet all day or by doing something strenuous? Do you receive purposeful or accidental exercise opportunities at work or are you just sitting in the same position all day? All these elements of your work routine will be important to consider as you decide which avenue of Intermittent Fasting to go down. You won't want to engage in a method like 20:4 if you're at work every day for incredibly short shifts. 20:4 works better for someone who works very long and distracting days. You won't want to try a method like 12:12 if part of your eating window involves being at work, when you're not allowed to eat at work. Remember to take your work life, routines, and restrictions into account when you go about making this choice, for you will make things much less harsh on yourself if you can look at this bigger picture from the beginning and planning stages.

Consider your friends, co-workers, and family:

How loud are their opinions? Are their lives oriented toward health? Do they demean you a lot or make fun of your choices? Or are they encouraging all the time? Are these people your support system or are they your devils' advocates? Do you have the sense that they want to see you succeed? On the most basic level, are they nice to you and respectful of your choices? It might not seem that important, but the attitudes and supportive capacity of your friends, co-workers, and family can mean the world when you make a big choice like starting Intermittent Fasting in your life. Sometimes, people just don't want to see us succeed. They block our successes with jealousy, pride, ignorance, or arrogance. When friends and family act like this, it's better to choose a method that allows you to avoid discussing IF around them whatsoever. When friends and family are open and supportive, they shouldn't influence your choice that much at all; it's just when things are tenuous that you'll need to keep them (and your time around them) in consideration.

Consider your dietary choices:

Do you eat a lot of processed foods? Or do you eat a largely whole-foods, plant-based diet? Do you count calories? Do you cautiously skim nutrition facts? Are you looking for something specific like high fat, high fiber, or high protein? Are you hoping to change your diet entirely or are you trying to keep things the way they are? Are you willing to sacrifice items of your diet to actualize your goals? All these questions help determine which type of method you're going to be ready for. Essentially, if you're trying to change your diet entirely, a method with days "on" and days "off" will work best for you. In this case, try 5:2, alternate-day, eat-stop-eat, and spontaneous skip methods.

However, if you don't want to change your diet that much at all, a method where you fast for periods within each day will be desirable instead. Try methods like 20:4, 16:8, 14:10, or 12:12 for this type of situation.

As long as you make your selection with these points in mind, you're sure to succeed with your Intermittent Fasting goals. You enable yourself to make the safest, smartest, best choice for your circumstances, and that's an incredible tool to use in so many different applications. In this case, it's a tool that will help keep you healthy, boost your brain, heal your heart, and shed that excess weight like melted butter!

Chapter 5: Effects of Intermittent Fasting

There are <u>pros and cons</u> of everything and intermittent fasting is no exception. It's a complete lifestyle change and hence making the transition can be difficult for some people. This section will help you in understanding how intermittent fasting can impact your health positively and the problems that you can face and how to deal with them.

Positive Impacts

Detoxification:

Whether you lose weight, or not, and how much weight you lose, is irrelevant inasmuch as the detoxing effect that intermittent fasting has on the body. You see, we accumulate toxins in our bodies over time. We tend to pick them up from food, air, drinks, and basically anything we come into contact with. These toxins enter the body and the immune system hacks away at them.

Generally speaking, the immune system will beat up toxins and rid the body of these harmful substances. However, the immune system needs certain freedom in order to function at full speed. Since the immune system is part of the overall human body machinery, it needs energy just like the other systems in the body.

Therefore, it essentially competes for energy. And when other systems in the body are overloaded, the immune system tends to become overwhelmed.

So, when the fasting process begins, the digestive tract begins to clear excess matter, including build up, until the digestive tract becomes clear of residue. This is part of the detoxification process. The body is now clearing waste that it doesn't need.

This process of clearing excess matter gives the immune system a chance to catch and fight off toxins as there are no new toxins coming in for a specific amount of time.

As the body begins to detox, the waste expelled from the organism allows organ systems to function better, the blood is improved, kidneys and liver function also improves, while high blood pressure may begin to dissipate. If this can be followed up with a balanced diet on non-fast days, then you could be setting yourself up for a dramatic turnaround which can leave you feeling like a million bucks.

Weight Loss:

The biggest reason why people engage in the intermittent fasting movement is because they are looking to lose weight. Well, first, I'd like to point out that losing weight is not the underlying intent of people who begin with intermittent fasting. Their true intention is to look better and feel better about themselves. And that does not necessarily imply that you need to lose weight.

In fact, crash diets have a habit of forcing the body to burn muscle instead of fat. So, dieters feel that the crash diet is working but in reality, all they are doing is changing their body composition. They are substituting lean muscle for fat. Naturally, muscle weighs more than fat. And so, the "benefits" are seen by the dieter.

But these results are not actually healthy results. They are simply a change in body composition which, in the end, leads to the rebound effect among other dietary conditions.

However, the intermittent fasting approach calls for the body to use up excess stores. This function is also improved when the individual is able to detox. So, the digestive system works much more efficiently. In turn, this kicks the metabolism into high gear giving it a chance to catch up.

Improved Blood Sugar Levels:

Speaking of blood sugar levels, intermittent fasting has been linked to improving blood sugar levels. While the data on this claim is still a bit sketchy, it seems to support the fact that the lack of caloric intake, especially sugars, will enable to body to detox and begin to process intake a lot better as compared to regular eating days.

This implies that the body is able to regular blood sugar to normal levels thereby reducing the overload that high amounts of sugar may cause on the body. In turn, this allows insulin production to level off and revert many of the adverse effects of having high blood sugar.

This regulatory effect allows the body to begin recovering its natural functions thereby improving overall wellness. Truth be told, high blood sugar levels are a real killer since they make it very hard for the body to level out hormonal function especially when insulin is out of whack. So, intermittent fasting is definitely an alternative for those folks who have

47

high blood sugar levels and are looking to improve their body's overall ability to process sugar.

Effect on High Blood Pressure:

Another interesting effect stemming from intermittent fasting is on high blood pressure.

In general, high blood pressure is associated with high levels of consumption in fat and sodium, that is, salt. When this happens, the body may trigger a reaction by elevating blood pressure in order to compensate for the constricted blood vessels.

Intermittent fasting, as has been stated, helps the body detox. And sodium (salt) is one of the most complex toxins in the body.

Sodium is soluble and water and is usually excreted in the urine. However, when sodium levels surpass the kidneys filtering capabilities, then one of the responses, in addition to water retention, is elevated blood pressure.

This condition will trigger the kidneys to work overtime in order to reduce the excess sodium in the body. This is where an individual may experience acute kidney failure, and if care is not taken, may lead to chronic kidney failure.

Effects on Heart Health:

Heart health is a complicated issue in today's world. We all want to be healthy and thrive, but the foods we eat and the activities we engage in often don't align with those goals, and those more immediate actions win out. In effect, many of our hearts aren't as healthy as they could be. Heart disease is still the biggest killer in the world to this day. However, the introduction of Intermittent Fasting into someone's lifestyle can greatly alter this potential, for it can reduce many risks associated with heart disease.

When it comes down to it, as long as one's Intermittent Fasting experience involves the reintroduction of electrolytes into the body, there's no potential harm posed to the heart whatsoever. There's only potential for growth, bolstering, and strengthening. However, without the right reintroduction of electrolytes, there is still the possibility of heart palpitations in individuals attempting IF. The heart needs electrolytes for its stability and efficacy, so as long as you drink a bit of salt with your water, your heart will only thank you!

Intermittent Fasting and Aging:

People love to talk about how Intermittent Fasting can reverse the effects of aging, and they're not wrong! The tricky part is elucidating the science behind the process they're referencing. The anti-aging potential tied up with Intermittent Fasting applies mostly to two things, your brain and, your whole body, through what's called *"autophagy"*. Overall, Intermittent Fasting heals the body through its ability to rejuvenate the cells. With this restricted caloric intake due to eating schedule or timing, the body's cells can function with less limitation and confusion while producing more energy for the body to use. In effect, the cells function more efficiently while the body can burn more fat and take in more oxygen for the organs and blood, encouraging the individual to live longer with increased sensations of "youth." Intermittent Fasting has been proven to keep the brain fit and agile. It improves overall cognitive function and memory capacity as well as cleverness, wit, and quick, clear thinking in the moment. Furthermore, Intermittent Fasting keeps the cells fit and agile through autophagy which is kick started by intermittent fasting where the cells are encouraged to clean themselves up and get rid of any "trash" that might be clogging up the works. By restricting your eating schedule a little bit each day (or each week), you can find your brain power boosted and your body ready for anything.

Side Effects

Headache:

It is the most common problem that people face. There is nothing to worry about the headaches as they occur when you are going through sugar withdrawal systems.

Our lifestyle has become such that our dependency on a carbohydrate-rich diet has increased a lot. We also keep consuming meals at frequent intervals and hence our body keeps getting glucose supply at short intervals. Our body loves glucose fuel as it is easy to burn and can be absorbed by the cells directly. However, being easy doesn't make it good. It leaves a lot of waste and residue in the body.

When you begin intermittent fasting, you block the regular supply of glucose fuel. Your body requires energy dump at short intervals. It can also derive energy from the fat stores but it is difficult to burn fuel and hence your brain starts giving you signals to eat frequently in the form of a headache. If you don't start eating frequently, your body would have no other option than to switch to fat fuel in the body. It is a clean fuel, leaves no toxic waste and residue. It would make you slimmer and also help in getting rid of diseases.

The easy way to counter the headaches is to have unsweetened black tea or coffee. These beverages help in dealing with the headache and also don't add any calorie to your system. You can have them without breaking your fast.

Hunger Pangs:

As we have already discussed in the book, the hunger pangs are a function of your biological clock. Even if you are feeling hungry it doesn't mean that you need to eat. The feeling of hunger is created by the release of a hormone called *Ghrelin*. The gut releases this hormone at times when you have food in a normal routine. It means that if you are habitual of eating at 8 in the morning or you eat immediately after brushing, you would feel the urge to eat at these times. The Ghrelin release is triggered by these signals. It wouldn't matter much that you had eaten a short while ago. The Ghrelin release is also triggered by time and incidents and not just by hunger. Now, because the hunger pangs are more dependent on signals than actual hunger they can be shifted easily. Another important thing about hunger pangs is that they are short. It means that if you are having hunger pangs, stomach cramps, and other such symptoms, you'll only need to hold on to it for a short while and they'll subside. Diverting your attention toward other important things is also a good way to avoid hunger pangs. Physical activities like walking, jogging and swimming can also help in subsiding hunger pangs. If you want, you can also drink unsweetened fresh lime water, black tea or coffee without sugar or water to fill your stomach and it would also help in suppressing the hunger. Very soon your gut will get used to the changed schedule and you will stop getting troubled by the hunger pangs.

Cravings:

Cravings can mean a lot of different things for men but they have a completely unique meaning when it comes to women. Food cravings can arise in women due to emotional needs or psychological distress too. Women can find great solace in food, especially in sweets and desserts.

However, craving, in general, is bad and the biggest cause of food craving is the intake of sweets. Candies, chocolates, cookies, carbonated beverages and other such things that are high in sugar content can cause sugar cravings. You must always try to stay away from such things.

There are several reasons because this happens:

- These things add lots of calories to your system and it can be counterproductive when you are trying to lose weight

- Most sweets have very high sugar content and low fiber. Although these things would give a signal to your system that a lot of calories are coming, your gut would get nothing in reality. However, the release of digestive juices would be there. It would harm your system seriously.

- The more sweets you eat, the faster you'll feel the need to eat again. Refined sugar is more addictive than most addictive substances in this world.

- High sugar foods would make you feel fuller very fast but they would also make you feel empty stomach with the same speed. This is highly confusing for your gut and your blood sugar control system also remains engaged unnecessarily.

The best way to deal with these problems is to abstain from high sugar foods completely. If possible staying away from high carb food items is also highly advisable as they also have a lot of sugar. You must try to avoid processed food items as much as possible.

Eat food items that are high in healthy fats and proteins. The higher the fat and protein content in your food, the lower will be your food cravings and these nutrients take a lot of time to get processed in the gut. Your gut remains pleasantly engaged and is able to clean itself properly.

Frequent Trips to the Toilet:

It is not very unusual for people to feel the frequent need to urinate when they begin their fasting routine. However, there is no need to worry as it is common for most weight loss programs. When you start any weight loss program and reduce your calorie intake, your body starts the protective mechanism.

It tries to lower energy needs. The water in your body apart from keeping you hydrated also helps in regulating the body temperature. However, as soon as you lower the calorie intake the body starts dumping the water to compensate for the energy deficit. But, there is nothing to worry as this is a temporary phenomenon and the water levels in your body would be back soon.

When you begin fasting your body also starts cleaning itself of the toxins and that also causes frequent urination. As long as you are not feeling any discomfort or the trips haven't increased a lot, it is not something that should worry you much.

You should keep drinking lots of water to compensate for the loss. If hypertension or other such medical issues are not there, you should even try having water with a pinch of sea salt. It helps in replenishing the loss of minerals that occurs due to excessive urination.

Binge Eating:

Once the fast is over, there are those who start eating and can't stop. With normal eating, they were able to control their appetite just fine, but with extended periods of not eating, their appetite seems insatiable. The inability to control appetite is a problem in itself. If the binge eating continues, the calories taken replace what has just been lost during the fast, and no weight will be lost despite all the effort. Worse still, more calories will be consumed than those lost, adding even more body fat.

Hyper-acidity:

The stomach contains acids which aid digestion. In the absence of food, you may feel stinging heartburn that could extend to the throat area. It is possible to experience heartburn during fasting that you previously did not experience at all.

Disrupted Sleep:

There are those who cannot sleep when hungry. Think about it; even in normal days, when you can sleep, you most probably end up in the kitchen taking a snack. A full stomach does encourage sleep, as all the energy is directed towards digesting the meal. You may have noticed that when you take a heavy lunch, you spend the afternoon feeling drowsy. An empty stomach could result in poor sleep, and you'll then spend the following day sleepy and fatigued.

Low Energy and Irritability:

Depending on how you are eating, your body may also be growing used to consuming fat as a fuel source rather than carbohydrates. So, in addition of losing its primary energy source, it is also have to switch how it consumes energy and where it comes from. This can lead to lowered energy for a while. The best thing to do during this time is to relax and keep your days as free as possible. Do things that exert the least amount of energy. If you are someone who regularly exercises and works out, reducing the amount that you work out or switching to a more relaxed workout like yoga can help you during the transition period.

In addition to feeling low energy, you may also feel irritability. Irritability is often caused by low energy and hunger. This may be frustrating early on as your body begins to adjust. Again, take it easy, reduce the amount of stress that you have in your daily life if possible, and give yourself time to adjust. Once you are used to your new eating habits the irritability will subside and your energy levels will pick up once again.

One common issue that people can have while beginning the fasting routine is a feeling of irritability. It isn't a permanent phenomenon and occurs only due to the fact that your blood sugar levels may fluctuate in the beginning. We have already discussed that your body may experience

55

low blood sugar levels for extended periods and that is not a very bad thing if you are not suffering from some chronic problem like diabetes. However, low blood sugar can cause irritability as the body is frantically looking for energy.

This is the stage where even your body is learning through the transition phase. It is making the switch to the fat fuel when it doesn't want to. This is a temporary phenomenon that wouldn't last very long.

Heartburn, Bloating, and Constipation:

Heartburn and bloating are common issues that you may face when you begin fasting. The reasons for bloating are simple, your gut keeps releasing the digestive juices at regular intervals but doesn't get anything to digest that causes the problem. However, this is a very temporary phenomenon as your gut would easily adjust to your new eating schedules and the problem would subside.

The heartburns are also part of the same process but they cause the most discomfort. The good thing is that they wouldn't last long. As soon as the release of digestive juices gets timed, bloating and heartburn would subside.

Constipation, on the other hand, can be a problem for many. The main reason for constipation isn't fasting but intake of improper food. It is a fact that your food intake may reduce when you begin intermittent fasting as your number of meals go down. However, if you don't include high fiber food items in your meals, your gut wouldn't have much to process. This can cause constipation that may trouble you a lot. The best way to avoid is to have fiber-rich food. Increase the salads and fiber-rich food in your meals and you would face no such issue. The important thing to remember is that you need to understand the problems you are facing and try to find the solution. Don't stick to a particular thing but try to find your best in the routine.

Intermittent fasting may become a big change in your life. You will have to make a few adjustments to welcome this change. It would be easy for you and even beneficial if you start making some adjustment to accommodate them. Don't be stubborn or a stickler for rules. Try to find your rhythm and flow with it.

Chapter 6: Tips and Tricks To Follow Correctly

Do you know what a fasting regime and New Year resolutions have in common? They start out great for a couple of months. First going to the second month; doing well. The third month; some hitches here and there. By the 6th or 7th month, some people have a problem remembering what their resolutions were in the first place. In this case, some will not remember their proposed fasting plans.

If you have fallen by the wayside, you'll be relieved to know you're not alone. Even the most enthusiastic fitness guru struggles with staying on course. If you have already missed a few steps, you can start all over again and get it right this time.

Sample these tips which will help you stay motivated:

Get an Accountability Partner

Having someone alongside you with similar goals can keep you on course. With the internet, your accountability partner can even be in another continent. The point here is that you're answerable to someone. You know what being answerable does to you? It makes you do things even when you don't feel like. Like when you don't feel like getting up and going to work, but you remember you have a boss to answer to, and you jump out of bed. The accountability partner for your fasting journey maybe your peer, but questions will still be asked. This also comes with a level of competition. If your partner can fast for 24 hours, or manage on a certain number of calories, why can't you? And who lost more pounds this week? You definitely don't want to be the one trailing, at least not every time. This accountability/competition relationship will ensure that you stay on track when you've have otherwise fallen off the radar. In fact, it is possible to achieve more with an accountability partner as opposed to a mentor. A mentor strikes an imposing figure, sort of talking down at you from a high horse. Accountability partners are at your level, demanding of you the much they demand of themselves.

Keep Informed

How much do you know about intermittent fasting? The more you know, the easier it will be for you to go through the process. Read blogs and watch videos to see what other women, and indeed men have to say about the fast. You'll realize that you're not alone in the issues you're experiencing.

This will also help you keep your expectations realistic. When it comes to weight loss, women can be impatient. A few days on a diet and you're already in front of the mirror looking for changes. Don't worry; we've all been there! You know by now that intermittent fasting is a way to lose weight fast; but how fast is fast? Getting the right information from those who have gone through the fast will let you know what to expect, and you'll be better prepared to deal with the process.

Set Goals with Rewards

Setting milestones with some goodies attached to them will keep you going even when your body and mind tells you otherwise. Keep in mind that the reward, in this case, is not food related.

Why can't you treat your sweet tooth as a reward? Well, to begin with, what you'd be saying to your mind is that the healthy foods you're eating are a punishment of sort, and only after eating them will you get some 'good' food.

Secondly, if you indulge in sugary and fatty treats, you'll only roll back on the gains already made. We don't want any of that, do we?

Your goal here is mainly weight loss, among other health gains. Once you've reached a goal of losing a certain number of pounds in a set time, you can treat yourself with a shopping trip for new clothes. Enjoy fitting in clothes that you would not have worn previously. As you look at yourself in the mirror and admire the new you, you'll be even more motivated to work towards your next goal.

Concentrate on Positive Feelings

How do you feel after shedding some pounds? I'm sure you're enjoying fitting into a smaller size of outfits, looking more presentable, feeling confident, being physically active without straining and so on.

Let these feelings color your day. Every time a thought crops up on how hungry you are, or how many foods you can no longer eat, remind yourself how dashing you look in that new dress. If you catch yourself staring at the clock gloomily counting how many more hours you have left on your fast, remind yourself that you can now make work presentations more confidently, presenting a positive body image.

Every time a negative feeling lingers, counter it with a positive thought and watch your energy revive.

61

Healthy-Eating Mind

Reprogram your mind to look at intermittent fasting, and indeed healthy eating as a whole as a positive lifestyle and not retribution. We're so accustomed to this random lifestyle where we eat what we want when we want it; that anything short of that feels like a punishment. Living healthy is choosing to be kind to your body, and knowing that it will remit the kindness right back. Think of your body for a moment as a separate entity from yourself. How would it feel when constantly being fed on the wrong foods that bring you terrible effects? How would it feel to constantly be fed on too much food and you have to strain to digest? If your body could speak, it could possibly ask these questions.

Feed it on the right foods, because it is the right thing to do. Give it just the right amount, without overloading it with unnecessary carbs, sugar, and fats. And give it a break from all the digesting work occasionally, who does not like a good rest?

Visualize the Future

Just picture how your future will turn out if you keep living this healthy lifestyle. You'll be disease-free, active, radiant and energetic. You'll improve your longevity, enjoying a longer, fuller life.

What's the other side of the coin? A life full of diseases. I'm sure you know such people, maybe even in your family, whose lives have been dimmed by disease. They're no longer able to do the things they enjoy. Their activity level is largely reduced if not cut off altogether. They are dependent on others to assist them even with minor roles. They carry medicine wherever they go. Isn't the idea of such a life horrifying, especially in a case where different choices were all was needed for a different turnout?

Choosing health is choosing life. If you still have the chance, this is an opportunity that you have to embrace. You work so hard to ensure your later days will see you age gracefully, do not let unhealthy living take this dream away from you.

Join a Community of Like Minds

Thank God for the internet; we can now form groups with people of similar interests even from different continents. Search the internet for women in intermittent fasting, and you should be able to find such groups. You can then exchange messages, photos, and videos of your progress. With a group also comes competition. We agree our bodies are different, but you definitely don't want to be the one trailing the lot by losing the least weight. That only helps you stay consistent. Share experiences, tips, goals, recipes, survival tactics and so on. Alone you can get discouraged and quit, but such a 'healthy living family' will not let you fall by the wayside.

Take Help of Positive Affirmations

Positive affirmations are very inspiring. They fill us with positive energy and help in clearing away negative thoughts. You can read positive affirmations, listen to them on the internet or recite them loudly. They help in every way. Positive affirmations keep your mind clear and give you the energy to sail through the bad times. They don't take much of your time and you also don't have to remain dependent on others. Taking help of positive affirmations is a great way to remain motivated.

Share Your Goals with Your Family and Friends

Sharing such things with others is always difficult. There is always the fear of being judged on the results. However, there are always some people in everyone's life who don't judge. It can be your parents, partner, siblings, or close friends. Share your goals with them and the problems you are facing in the way. Discuss with them the ways to get out of the problems. They can give you suggestions or at least lend their ears. Even letting it off your chest is also a great relief most of the times.

You will always have an assurance that there are people who really understand your efforts and are supporting you in them. It is not necessary that you disclose your goals to everyone but sharing it with some of your very close people is always a good idea.

Professional Help

Obesity is not a rare problem these days. In fact, it is one of the most common ailments faced by people. Therefore, you can also get several professionals with whom you can discuss your problems and progress. You can consult your doctor and periodically discuss your progress. This serves two purposes. First, there will be a professional to guide you about the progress. You will get professional opinions on time about the problems you face on your way. You can get tips on nutrition and also advice about the ways to improve the progress.

Support Groups

It is a cost-effective way to get help. Support groups can emerge as pillars of strength. There are many people suffering from the same problems. They are also going through the same trials and tribulations. They can prove to be a great help in case you need moral or mental support. Most of the people in support groups are facing similar problems and hence your problems can be common. You can get the tips that worked for them. Such support groups can be of great help.

Keep the Atmosphere at Your Home Conducive

Most of the time, the atmosphere around us makes our efforts difficult. For instance, if your fridge is full of carbonated beverages, fast food snacks and munchies, it would be difficult to control the urge to eat. If people in your home are casually eating things all the time, you would start feeling punished and left out. It is important that you explain your goals and make arrangements so that the process gets simpler and not difficult. It is important that you clear your fridge. If it is shared by others then you should limit your access to the fridge. Your kitchen should be stacked with healthy things and junk food should be removed so that you don't get tempted and eat it.

Remove all kinds of sweets and chocolates from your home. They are irresistible and can break your will in your weak moments.

By thinking of losing weight you have already cleared the first hurdle. You only need to become more conscious of your choices to succeed in your efforts.

Chapter 7: What Foods & Liquids Do

When you go about your first round of intermittent fasting, you'll need to know what to avoid and what to keep close at hand.

When it comes to foods, the best things to have around <u>are</u>:

All Legumes and Beans – good carbs can help lower body weight without planned calorie restriction

Anything high in protein – helpful in keeping your energy levels up in your efforts as a whole, even when you're in a period of fasting

Anything with the herbs cayenne pepper, psyllium, or dried/crushed dandelion – they'll contribute to weight loss without sacrificing calories or effort

Avocado – a high-, good-calorie fruit that has a lot of healthy fats

Berries – often high in antioxidants and vitamin C as well as flavonoids for weight loss

Cruciferous Vegetables – broccoli, cauliflower, brussel sprouts, and more are incredibly high in fiber, which you'll definitely want to keep constipation at bay with IF

Eggs – high in protein and great for building muscle during IF periods

Nuts & Grains – sources of healthy fats and essential fiber

Potatoes – when prepared in healthy ways, they satiate hunger well and help with weight loss

Wild-Caught Fish – high in healthy fats while providing protein and vitamin D for your brain

When it comes to liquids, some of it is pretty self-explanatory:

- *Water* - It's always good for you! It will help keep you hydrated, it will provide relief with headaches or light headedness or fatigue, and it clears out your system in the initial detox period.

Try adding a squeeze of lemon, some cucumber or strawberry slices, or a couple of sprigs of mint, lavender, or basil to give your water some flavor if you're not enthused with the taste of it plain.

If you need something else to drink, you can seek out:

- *Probiotic drinks like kefir or kombucha*

You can even look for probiotic foods such *as sauerkraut, kimchi, miso, pickles, yogurt, tempeh*, and more!

- *Probiotics* work amazingly well at healing your gut especially in times of intense transition, as with the start of intermittent fasting.

- *Black coffee,* whenever possible, in moderation

Sweeteners and milk aren't productive for your fasting and weight loss goals.

- Heated or chilled *vegetables* or bone broths

- *Teas* of any kind

- *Apple cider vinegar* shots

Instead, try water or other drinks with ACV mixed in.

Drinks to avoid would be:

- *Regular soda*

- *Diet soda*

- *Alcohol* of any kind

- *High-sugar coconut and almond drinks*

- i.e. *coconut water, coconut milk, almond milk*, etc.

- *Anything with artificial sweetener* will shock your insulin levels into imbalance with your blood sugar later on

Go for the low-sugar or unsweetened milk alternative if it's available.

Focus on Healthy Food

The human body needs macronutrients, minerals, and vitamins to function properly. All of them can be found in food, but unfortunately, the food available nowadays is not very consistent in nutrients. Most of the food we eat today is processed, and the more processed food is, the unhealthier and less consistent in nutrients. Also, processed food is rich in carbs, a macronutrient which can cause terrible effects to the human body. In fact, food has killed more people over the last few decades than drugs, alcohol, and cigarettes put together. Around 70% of the diseases known today are caused by food. You are probably asking yourself why this happens. The answer lies with processed foods and carbs, as they are the roots of all these problems. Carbs can be split into sugar and starch, and sugar really needs no introduction, as it's perhaps the most harmful substance ever to be consumed by humans. Without any doubt, food was a lot healthier 100 years ago, and there weren't so many cases of obesity and diabetes (both caused by an excess of carbs). The problem with sugar is that we consume it voluntarily and even feed it to our children. This kind of food causes addiction, as you will not feel satiety for a long time (in fact, you will feel hungry sooner), it won't cover the body's nutritional needs and you will crave some more carbs very soon. Those carbs contain glucose, which can be used by the body to generate energy, but this energy is produced only through physical exercise. The glucose doesn't get consumed and instead gets stored in your blood, raising your insulin and blood sugar levels. This is one step closer to diabetes, so this is how it all gets started.

Most of the food we consume today is processed and even what it claims to be natural is not organic. Before being able to process food, the most processed food you can dream of was bread, but the recipe was pretty simplistic, so different than the bread we are consuming today. Food was cooked from natural ingredients, and it had great nutritional value. Also, the lifestyle was a lot more active, as there weren't too many means of transportation back then. When we think of natural food nowadays, it's simply very difficult to find organic food, as chemicals are used to grow fruits, vegetables or crops. Fertilizers are no longer natural (with high chemical content), and animals are being fed concentrated food to grow incredibly fast. The meat we are consuming comes from these animals, and if they are fed this kind of food, this will affect us. Processing food is all about adding extra value to the product, otherwise, companies operating in this domain can't seem to find a way to increase their profits. It's fair to say that for the sake of profits, food processing companies are literally making poison to be consumed by the people. Everything which is packed and has more ingredients (many of them being chemicals you can't even pronounce) is processed food. This type of food is promoted by supermarkets and fast-food restaurants, as it fits perfectly with the current way of life. Finding healthy food is becoming a challenge nowadays, especially for the people who want to cut down on carbs. You are probably wondering what exactly you can eat in order to stay away from carbs.

Intermittent fasting is a procedure of self-discipline, in which you impose on yourself a strict set of rules and eat only within the designated feeding window. For most of the programs, there is no mention of what you can eat. However, this doesn't mean that you can stuff yourself with junk food. Healthy food can improve the results of this program, and there are a few options when it comes to healthy diets. You can consider a keto diet, a Mediterranean diet or an alkaline diet, and they all involve consuming plenty of vegetables and less meat. Most of them are LCHF (low carb high fat) diets, but the protein intake may vary from one diet to another. This diet traces its roots from the living habits of the people living in the Mediterranean basin, so it doesn't mean just Italian cuisine. But be careful, as this diet doesn't include pizza and it doesn't focus on pasta. This kind of diet has its very own food pyramid, based on how frequent you should try that food type.

If the standard food pyramid has **6 different levels**:

1) *Vegetables, salad, fruits*

2) *Bread, whole-grain cereals, pasta, potatoes, and rice* - the food category richest in carbs

3) *Milk, yogurt and cheese*

4) *Meat, poultry, fish, eggs, beans, and nuts*

5) *Oils, spread, and fats*

6) *Sweets, snacks, soft drinks, juices* - basically food and drinks with very high levels of sugar and salt

The <u>Mediterranean diet</u> has it figured differently, as you can see below:

1) The base of the pyramid is represented by the *physical activity*, as this is a lifestyle for people living in the Mediterranean region.

2) The second level of the pyramid includes different types of food like *fruits, vegetables, beans, nuts, olive oil, seeds and legumes, herbs and spices, but also grains* (with a focus on whole grains). Most of the foods on this level should be consumed on a daily basis.

3) The third level of the pyramid is represented by *seafood and fish*, which should be consumed approximately twice a week.

4) The next level features poultry, *cheese, yogurt, and eggs.*

5) The last level of the pyramid is represented by *meat and sweets.*

The logic behind this pyramid is the same as with the standard food pyramid, the more necessary the food type is, the lower is on the pyramid. The Mediterranean diet includes a plethora of food types to choose from, all healthy, delicious and nutritious. Therefore, it's probably the most complete meal plan you can associate with intermittent fasting. You can eat fish, seafood, meat, chicken, turkey, but most of all, you will need to consume veggies, fruits, seeds, nuts, dairy products, and also olive oil. This diet focuses on healthy unsaturated fats, so it's exactly what the body needs for the IF lifestyle, as it can bring your body into ketosis (the metabolic state when ketones are multiplying to break down the fat tissue).

Some of the main features of the Mediterranean diet are:

- Focus on the consumption of *fruits, nuts, veggies, legumes, and whole grains*

- There is also a high emphasis on consuming healthy fats from *canola or olive oil*

- Forget about the use of salt to flavor your food, as this diet encourages the use of herbs and spices

- Less red meat (pork or beef) and more *fish or chicken/turkey*

- You can even *drink red wine* in moderate quantities

It doesn't sound like a diet at all, as there are so many types of food accepted. It's more of a lifestyle than a meal plan. If a standard diet is something you need to stick to for a few weeks, the Mediterranean diet is the meal plan that you have to stick to for the rest of your life. It can include all 3 meals of the day, but you can also have snacks or desserts. It sounds too good to be true? Well, this is what the Mediterranean diet is, and it can work wonders on you if you combine it with intermittent fasting and working out. But, that's not all! By now you already know the benefits of intermittent fasting. How about adding some more benefits by following this type of diet? If you want stronger bones, lower risk of frailty, lung disease or heart disease, and even to ward off depression, then you definitely need to try this diet.

Since this meal plan is diversified, you don't have to make radical changes in your refrigerator, as you are probably already consuming some of the foods mentioned here. However, at least when it comes to veggies, legumes, and fruits, you will need to eat them fresh, so frequent shopping may be required.

You need to know that the ingredients of the Mediterranean diet are structured into **11 categories**, as you can see below:

1) *Vegetables* are one of the most important categories included in this meal plan and you can consume them frozen or fresh. In the frozen veggies group there can be included peas, green beans, spinach or others. In terms of fresh vegetables, you can buy tomatoes, cucumbers, peppers, onions, okra, green beans, zucchini, garlic, peas, cauliflower, mushrooms, broccoli, potatoes, peas, carrots, celery leaves, cabbage, spinach, beets, or romaine lettuce.

2) The *fruits* you need to include in your shopping list are peaches, pears, figs, apricots, apples, oranges, tangerines, lemons, cherries, and watermelon.

3) You can't have a Mediterranean diet without some *high-fat* dairy *products*. Milk (whether is whole or semi-skimmed) is no longer considered a good option, as it also has a higher concentration of carbs. You can buy instead sheep's milk yogurt, Greek yogurt, feta cheese, ricotta (or other types of fresh cheese), mozzarella, groviera, and mizithra.

4) This diet doesn't focus too much on *meat or poultry*, but you can still eat them twice a week. Your shopping list will need to include chicken (whether you prefer it whole, breasts or thighs), pork, ground beef, and veal. This is where you can get most of your proteins from, but still, you need to keep the protein intake at a low level.

5) Can you imagine a Mediterranean diet without *fish or seafood*? This food is a must in this meal plan, although you can only have it twice a week. So, you will need to buy salmon, tuna, cod, sardines, anchovies, shrimp, octopus or calamari. You can eat some of them fresh or canned.

6) Although you don't have to abuse them, your shopping list should definitely include *bread or pasta.* If they are made from whole grains are even better, as they are the right choice in this case. Try to avoid the unnecessary consumption of pastry, like having bagels, pretzels or croissants with your coffee. You can eat and buy instead whole grains bread, paximadi (barley rusks), breadsticks (also made from whole grains), pita bread, phyllo, pasta, rice, egg pasta, bulgur, and couscous.

7) Your shopping list must include *healthy fats and nuts*. Olive oil should be consumed on a daily basis, so you need to have it in your household. Also, in terms of nuts, it's recommended that you buy tahini, almonds, walnuts, pine nuts, pistachios, and sesame seeds.

8) *Beans* are an important part of this diet, so you definitely need to buy lentils, white beans chickpeas, and fava.

9) *Pantry items* are the miscellaneous part of this meal plan. In this group, you can include olives, canned tomatoes, tomato paste, sun-dried tomatoes, capers, herbal tea, honey, balsamic or red wine vinegar and wine (preferably red).

10) As mentioned above, *herbs and spices* are used for flavoring your food. As this diet involves a lot of home cooking, having plenty of spices and herbs can make a difference. That's why your shopping list must include herbs and spices like oregano, mint, dill, parsley, cumin, basil, sea salt, black pepper, cinnamon, sea salt and all kind of spices.

11) You definitely need to buy some *greens*, like chicory, dandelion, beet greens and amaranth and include them in your meal plan.

Calories Management

The first and perhaps one of the most important parts of successfully eating the intermittent fasting diet without any serious side effects is maintaining a proper calorie count each day. Having a smaller eating window can make this more challenging, so it is important that you are eating properly during these windows.

If you begin eating the intermittent fasting diet and do not receive enough calories, the impacts that you might experience could be quite negative. In addition to experiencing things like excessive hunger and headaches, you may also begin experiencing excessive weight loss. Weight loss on the intermittent fasting diet is a great side effect, but not if it is happening because you are quite literally starving.

It is important that you discover what the healthy calorie intake is for your age and weight range. Then, make sure that you are incorporating that caloric intake into your eating window. This may mean that during your eating window you are eating fairly consistently in order to get in enough calories to remain healthy. Focus on eating calorie-dense foods that are high in nutrition, such as meats and vegetables, to get your intake up. This will ensure that you stay well-nourished and that you do not begin losing weight as a result of starvation.

Lowered Carbs Intake:

Many people who realize that they need to increase their calorie intake in a short amount of time may look towards pasta and other carbs for their caloric value. Unfortunately, pasta and other carbohydrates are not ideal when it comes to using the intermittent fasting diet. They lack a rich nutritional value and are more likely to increase weight gain, elevate blood sugars, and cause bloating and constipation, especially if they are a primary food that you consume to attempt to reach your caloric intake through carbs.

In addition to their ability to spike your blood sugars, carbs also cause other side effects that can make intermittent fasting more challenging.

For example, you might find that you are irritable and more tired when you consume a high level of carbs each day. You might also find that you struggle concentrating and that getting through your fasting cycles is more of a challenge. You can avoid these side effects by reducing carbs in your diet.

When you are intermittently fasting, a good idea is to avoid high carb intake altogether. Eating a low carb or ketogenic diet can support you in getting all of the nutrition that you need without consuming carbohydrates as a filler. This will not only support you in avoiding the unwanted side effects but will also ensure that you are gaining the maximum value of your diet. Lowering your carbohydrates will actually increase the level of ketones in your body, making it even easier for you to experience increased energy, weight loss, and muscle gain.

Increased Healthy Fats:

Since the intermittent diet increases ketones in your body, you want to increase healthy fats in your diet. Ketones are responsible for supporting your body in using fat as a fuel instead of sugars. This means that you need to have a healthy amount of fats for the ketones to effectively work on your body. This might seem counterintuitive since you want to burn fats, but it is actually essential. You need to provide your body with enough fuel to help it maintain itself and stay functioning and healthy.

Increasing your intake of healthy fats throughout your eating windows can support your body in having plenty of fats to produce energy from. It is important that you choose healthy fats for this, as this will keep your fuel clean and effective. Filling up on unhealthy fats can be dangerous as it can actually have a negative impact on heart and blood health. Fats like the ones you get from avocado oil and coconut oil, nuts and seeds, fish, and cheeses can support you in maintaining your energy and staying healthy while eating the intermittent fasting diet. I have included a list of healthy fats below to give you an idea of what to look for and where to start.

Avoiding Sugary and Starchy Foods:

Sugary and starchy foods should be avoided in any diet. They can reduce metabolic efficiency and cause blood sugar spikes. When you are intermittently fasting, avoiding these types of foods can help you maintain your overall health. It can also support you in reducing negative side effects during your fasting cycles.

Ideally, you want to avoid sugars in any variety. This means that you should lower the amount of processed sugars and sweets that you eat, as well as reduce the amount of fruit you eat. If you are going to eat something sweet, however, opt for fruits over processed sugars. This will ensure that you are maintaining healthy blood sugar levels. This will also help your body continue using ketones and fat as fuel instead of sugar and carbs. In the end, you will get better results from your diet.

Starches can also break down and become sugars in the body, so it is important to avoid these, too. This means avoiding things like potatoes, corn, peas, rice, and beans. That way, your body can continue operating optimally and you get the best results from your diet.

Chapter 8: Hormonal Regulation And How Its Impacted By Intermittent Fasting

Hormonal regulation is a significant benefit of intermittent fasting. Women, in particular benefit from the effects of fasting, especially when it involves stabilizing certain hormones while increasing or decreasing other hormones. There are several ways in which intermittent can regulate hormone production. One of the most significant advantages of fasting is the reversal of insulin resistance. When the body sugar levels rise consistently, this increases glucose, and creates a resistance to insulin. Periods of fasting, both short and long terms, help the body regain the normal, healthy level of sensitivity towards insulin. This has the effect of regulating insulin, which is a hormone, and helps prevent to onset of type 2 diabetes. Growth hormones are important for helping the body burn fat and build muscle. During periods of intermittent fasting, growth hormones increase significantly, which helps accelerate weight loss and build muscle mass.

How Intermittent Fasting Affects Women Differently Than Men

Women of all ages benefit from intermittent fasting, from early 20s, through perimenopause, menopause and into senior years. There are emerging studies and results that show a different impact on women and men, when it comes to the impact of intermittent fasting. One of the major reasons for this difference is how women's bodies are more adapted to storing fat, which is significantly changed once weight loss begins during fasting. Low to zero calorie intake during a fast can cause side effects in some women, such as cramps and changes in menstruation. This can occur with prolonged fasting, though most side effects or discomfort associated with cessation of food is temporary, for both men and women.

The **advantages** of intermittent fasting for women are significant, and are often directly connected to hormones and their production:

- Lower insulin levels in women keep blood sugar low on a consistent basis. This occurs after only a few weeks of regular intermittent fasting. This seems to remain consistent in the long term, with overall changes in insulin at normal levels.

- Inflammation is reduced, and specifically inflammation and weight gain associated with chronic conditions showed significant improvement over time. As chronic inflammation can cause weight gain, this also results in weight maintenance, in addition to weight loss.

- Depression affects a lot of people, which can trigger other habits, such as overeating and not getting regular exercise. One study noted that after eight weeks of intermittent fasting, there was a noticeable decline in depression. This affects a lot of women during different stages of life: post-partum, perimenopause, and during menstrual cycles. While it is not advised to practice intermittent fasting during pregnancy or while breastfeeding, eating healthy, nutritious meals is a good way to get everything you need, until you are ready to start a fasting method.

- Women more than men, lose bone mass as they age. Preserving muscle mass is of utmost importance at all stages in life, though more so in advanced age. Restricting calories through fasting, rather than calorie restricted diets that do not include fasts in the plan, show a better retention of muscle mass. This helps the body break down fat and aids in weight loss.

While all fasting methods are beneficial for women, some studies indicate that regular use of certain fasting programs <u>are ideal</u>:

- *24-hour fasting, done twice each week*

- *16:8 and 18:6 fasting methods*

- *5:2 fasting*

IF & the Female Body

Since intermittent fasting is not so much a diet as it is an altered pattern in eating times and frequency, its relationship with the female body is not the same as the standard diet's relationship would be. In fact, it's not necessarily supportive for females to practice a strict diet while intermittent fasting, for the combination of the two, can work serious havoc on the female body itself.

To counteract any curious side-effects of IF on your physical and mental states, you can try and make sure to eat as nutritious a selection of food as you can, whenever possible. Furthermore, you can try not to overexert yourself through exercise, especially since you're altering your food and nutrition intake significantly. Also, you can ensure that you're not forcing yourself to engage in IF if you're ill, suffering from an infection, or struggling with a chronic disorder of some kind. Finally, if your body is exhausted due to work or struggles with anxiety (or otherwise), you might not want to put yourself through additional stress with a new pattern of eating.

The most important thing to do as you begin to engage with intermittent fasting as a female-bodied person is to make sure you're as connected to (and introspective of) your body as you can be, as often as you're able to be. The more you know your body and its tendencies (i.e. the frequency of your period, your tendencies with metabolism, your fat storage areas, your most common moods, your emotional crutches, etc.), the more successful your experiences with intermittent fasting can be.

Physical Effects of IF for Women

While the general effects of intermittent fasting include increased energy overall, clearer cognition and memory, improved immunity, slowed aging process, better heart health, increased insulin sensitivity, and more, are some of the physical effects for women deserve a little more detail in specific.

For women, it **includes**:

- Lowered blood pressure in about two months or less, lowered cholesterol by ¼ the original toxic amount, better blood sugar control, decreased likelihood for type 2 diabetes, lowered chances of cancer, potential for increased muscle mass (with the ability to preserve it longer!), increased lifespan by up to 50 years, and increased awareness of internal bodily processes in general.

- After a few months of intermittent fasting practice, you're sure to feel that your senses are somewhat heightened compared to how they were before, that your body works better and smoother than ever, that your weight melts off like wax from a candle, and that your mind and cognition are clearer than ever before.

- Some physical effects function almost like warning signs for the woman practicing IF, too. If you experience poorer skin conditions, complete insomnia, loss of hair, excessive or shocking decrease in muscle mass, loss of period entirely, heart arrhythmia, or increased inflammations (whether internally or externally), you'll definitely want to consider altering your process, stopping the IF for a while, or visiting a nearby doctor for advice.

Using IF to Help with Periods, Fertility, and Metabolism

If you struggle monthly through painful periods; if you know you don't want to have children and you're not concerned about future fertility; or if you want to kick-start your metabolism to help yourself lose weight, all you have to do is start intermittently fasting without any concern whatsoever. If you're looking for hard and fast changes for your harsh menses, your fertility, or your weight issues, work your way up to fasting a few days a week, and you're sure to see the side-effects you seek played out within a month or two.

85

If you're interested in getting help with painful periods without substantial effects on your future fertility, simply make sure to get enough fat in your diet and supplemental estrogen (which you can find over the counter in a variety of forms). By making sure to consume enough healthy fat and by not restricting your caloric intake too much, you can use intermittent fasting to ease difficult menses without it having too much effect on your metabolism at the moment, and with it having hardly any effect on your fertility later on.

If you want the metabolism boost without effect on your periods or fertility, here's what you can do. Make sure you're eating enough healthy fats, but restrict caloric intake slightly, not too much though, mind you! You don't want to hurt those hunger hormones or inhibit your ability to ovulate and have a healthy period!

For these reasons, you should make sure not to intentionally or fastidiously "diet" while you're intermittently fasting but seeing as how you do want to lose weight and kick-start that metabolism, you can do something to help your body remember not to hang onto too much excess! That "something" that works so well is two-part: (1) once you define your method, keep to its timing strictly and; (2) when you have your meals, don't overindulge, binge, or gorge yourself; allow your caloric intake to be limited, but only slightly, as you work with IF.

Chapter 9: Intermittent Fasting For Weight Loss

Learn About Your Natural Eating Pattern

The first step towards any change in diet is *awareness*. Start paying attention to what you're eating and begin being conscious of your dietary choices.

The best way to keep track of them is to write them down in a small notebook. Carry a pen and paper or make notes in an app on your phone or tablet about when and what you eat. Most people are shocked by how much they eat in a day. Identifying personal eating patterns and the types of foods preferred is the appropriate place to start when embarking on intermittent fasting.

Create a food journal or log (you will find a link in bonus section to get a copy of a free printable food journal) that includes **the following items**:

- *Log the Date and day of the week*: Note whether it's morning, noon, or night. You'll have to be time-specific when you start fasting.

- *What are all the foods and drinks consumed*: List the types, amounts, and whether you added calories through use of condiments, butter, sugar, etc. Beverages count, so make note of them too. Keep notes on what you add to your beverages, such as sugar or honey as a sweetener. This will be important later.

- *Portion sizes*: Estimates of the volume, weight or number of items works just fine. If you prefer to measure, that's great as well. The point is to get a sense of quantity.

- *The location of your meals*: Take notes of where you are at mealtimes. Are you in a car, at a desk, or on a couch? Are you eating alone or with other people?

- *What is your activity level while eating*: Pay attention to what you are focused on as you're eating food. Are you browsing the internet or checking Instagram, or simply talking with friends?

- *How are you feeling*: What are your emotions? Are you happy, excited, depressed, stressed, anxious, or content? Our emotions can direct our eating choices, and conversely, eating can inspire emotions. Pay particular attention to increases in eating based on emotional situations.

To make your food journal valuable, be open and honest. Take the time to note every bite of food eaten and beverage you drink. If you don't log everything, you won't have an accurate picture of your dietary habits. For the most accurate results, try to record your food intake within 15 minutes of the time you eat.

Intermittent Fasting and Exercise

Myths still exist that caution people away from getting involved in any type of exercise program or physical training during periods of intermittent fasting. Although it's true that your body will not perform well for an extended period of time on empty, but true intermittent fasting is not about complete deprivation. It is periodic, scheduled time away from food that lasts for mere hours.

As long as you follow the correct methods for intermittent fasting and eat right during your window of nutritional opportunity, you can use exercise routines to increase the power output of your body. Running lean means a more efficient firing of your internal engine.

Transition Slowly

Think of your first month of intermittent fasting as an experiment, rather than a difficult task you must do in order to be healthy. Just relax and break it down into small, manageable tasks you know you can accomplish. When you're ready, consider increasing the number of days in the week that you fast for 14-hours, or consider fasting longer on the days of the week you choose to fast. See below for an example of how to build on the plan described above by adding a 15-hour fasting period to your schedule.

Learn to Listen to Your Body

Observe how your body responds and think about anything that comes up. The goal is learning from this process and finding a way to do it that works for you. If you start to feel hunger cravings or like you are depriving yourself without cause, return to the reasons why you decided to try intermittent fasting and revisit the benefits. It's a good idea to avoid snacks. Keep this principle at the front of your mind as you begin exploring how to incorporate intermittent fasting into your life. The goal is to eat consciously and that often means breaking old eating habits that no longer serve us.

Symptoms You Should Watch for

If you don't feel well, do not delay breakfast, even if it is the first time you are trying intermittent fasting. If you skipped dinner the night before, and wake up not feeling well, eat something simple. If you need to eat breakfast at 7 am, give yourself permission to do so this time. It's not a problem. That's 12-hours out of 24, and it's a fine place to start. All you had to do was get through the tough time after dinner, go to bed, and wake up.

It's ideal to have an open and honest discussion with your physician before embarking on the intermittent fasting diet. You should always heed their advice if you have any underlying medical conditions or take prescription medications.

Certain medicines can interfere with the effectiveness of this diet regime. And, most importantly, if you are ill, or begin to feel sick, stop fasting.

Chapter 10: Intermittent Fasting And Other Diets

There are many different ways to construct your diet. All the fads that come and go may seem suitable for a week or two but often fall short on results and fulfillment. When seeking to improve your diet look to time-tested meal plans, find the ones based on distinct cultures or with a rich history of being locally sourced. You can make your choices for your diet, you can have some days that are vegetarian and some days that are not, there really are no official rules for diet except what you find to be fitting and what works for you. Be creative and open-minded in choosing meal plans.

We will now explore popular diets that also conform to the standards of an intermittent fasting routine. These diets are in no way the only paths to take when choosing a diet but we selected these diets to reflect ideal examples for intermittent fasting practices. We must keep in mind the importance of listening to our bodies and how they react to different diets. If you're unsure about a certain diet, simply test it out for a few days or weeks.

Let's look at **these diets** below:

Raw Food Diet

This diet is relatively self-explanatory. The guidelines are simple: eat only raw foods. Many people seeking to adhere to this diet gradually introduce raw foods into their usual diet until they feel comfortable with a completely raw diet. And when we say raw, that's strictly what we mean.

These are uncooked and unprocessed foods. No dehydration or preservation but raw, fresh foods, often times not even seasoned with salt. While the nutritional value is not up for debate, the raw diet can be a bit limiting.

You will need consistent access to fresh foods and would typically find it tough to dine with friends who aren't adhering to a raw diet. This structure is probably the toughest to uphold with the least amount of options available.

A raw shopping list would look like this:

- *Nuts*

- *Seeds*

- *Fruits*

- *Vegetables*

- *Smoothies* and salads rule this diet

It is tough to fill yourself on raw foods successfully, not to mention it can be costly to supply because it is nothing but fresh foods from day to day.

This diet acts as a great way to cleanse and experiment with but rarely is it practiced for lifelong periods of time aside from a minority of people.

Paleo Diet

The paleo diet has seen very positive responses from weight lifting communities as well as those seeking a diet that is rich in cultural history. The paleo diet is based on what we now believe that our ancestors ate during hunter-gatherer eras. These were the times before agriculture saw plenty of meat being consumed as well as raw nuts, seeds, and berries. Some may even feel inclined to actually forage for the foods or hunt for their meat sources. Scientific studies show insight into these times, suggesting that our ancestors were very active and essentially maintained a mostly raw diet, and more interestingly, may have fasted during times of unsuccessful hunts or forages. There is a common misconception that prehistoric man ate nothing but meat. This is up for debate but the majority of experts suggest that the inconsistency of hunts and large tribe size would mean that less than half of the diet would consist of meat. This could vary greatly in different regions of the world and with the mysterious nature of our past, it is tough to accurately suggest how our ancestors lived. We can safely assume that they ate a diet high in protein and fiber, with very little caloric intake, here we see that this concept fits nicely into intermittent fasting practices.

While the paleo diet has varying philosophies person to person, the structure is pretty consistent. Although pinpointing the exact diet of past generations is an ill-fated task, we can give a loose guideline for what is today considered a paleo diet.

It is <u>as it follows</u>:

- *Lean meats and seafood*

- *Eggs*

- *Root vegetables*

- *Seeds*

- *Nuts*

- *Fruits*

- *Oils such as olive or coconut*

- *Herbs*

This is not a comprehensive list but a solid beginner's guide to starting to work with a paleo style diet. Keep in mind these ingredients would be wild foraged or trapped and hunted on the day of consumption. The fresher the ingredient, the closer to a legitimate paleo diet it is. There are also many foods avoided by adherents of the paleo diet. Consider that agriculture and farming wouldn't have existed, so many foods that are available and popular in our society today would not be accessible.

Some examples include:

- *Legumes*

- *Grains*

- *Dairy Products*

- *Processed oils*

- *Processed sweeteners*

- *Any processed or frozen food*

Whole Thirty Diet

Rising in popularity in recent years with the many diagnoses of celiac and other gluten intolerances, the whole thirty diet requires one to give up foods that are common allergies for many people. The idea that these foods are the cause of humans developing the allergies is at the heart of this diet. These foods are seen as undesirable for adherents of this diet. The practice of this diet itself asks that you do a thirty-day clean eating, cutting out these undesirable foods to see if you feel noticeably better due to an acute allergy to these common culprits.

The **foods** often <u>excluded</u> are as follows:

- *Peanuts*

- *Beans*

- *Grains, even gluten-free grains and other sources of gluten*

- *Shellfish*

- *Dairy*

- *Soy*

- *Nuts*

- *Seeds*

This list is certainly doesn't include every allergy causing food. If you suspect a food may be causing harmful reactions, cut it out during the clean eating cycle and see what happens. Upon gradually introducing these foods, you can take note of your body's reactions or lack thereof.

The whole thirty diet is a great diet for practicing awareness of our bodies. This diet can help us develop our skills and habits of listening to our bodies. By individually reintroducing foods after a type of cleanse, we can better learn how certain types of foods react when we ingest them. This makes the whole thirty diet ideal for preparing for intermittent fasting. Start the whole thirty diet about one month before a fasting week to ease into the IF mindset and prepare your body for dietary changes.

Vegetarian Diets

Plant-based diets are incredibly popular not only because of the internet and globalization but also many cultures have sustained a plant-based standard for millennia. Vegetarianism has seen incredible success in changing people's lives for the better, it is popular throughout the world, comprising over twenty percent of the entire population.

Many people are attracted to vegetarian diets to help counteract the western world's reliance on meat and animal products. Farming industries contribute to increase the world's pollution and deforestation problems so, with its health benefits and ecological awareness, vegetarianism acts a powerful diet to change your life on the individual level and your surrounding world.

Vegetarian guidelines are simple to follow. You essentially do not include any meat into your diet. This could mean many different things to many different people. Some people exclude meat itself but eat eggs and use animal-based broths. Other vegetarians exclude any animal products; so no dairy, broths, milk, or eggs. This more strict diet can borderline a vegan diet, but veganism tends to be stricter, promoting animal rights activism. Vegetarian diets usually include cheeses and dairy but it would be on only certain occasions.

The vegetarian diet is great for those who want a simple change to improve their diet, some people choose one day a week to each vegetarian; others explore the diet thoroughly, often taking in the eating habits for the rest of their lives.

Vegetarian ingredients would look like the following list:

- *Vegetables*

- *Fruits*

- *Nuts*

- *Seeds*

- *Berries*

- *Whole Grains*

- *Dairy*

- *Eggs*

- *Beans*

- *Soy or Tofu*

Vegan Diet

Adopting a vegan diet is similar to a vegetarian one, only vegans are strictly plant-based. It doesn't include any animal products at all. No dairy, no broths, no eggs, honey, and not even using make-up or wearing clothes made of animal products. We see here that this diet comes equipped with a philosophy. Animal activism is a crucial aspect of veganism. Many vegans protest the farming industry and even denounce domestication of animals. Social philosophy is not the intention of this book so we will leave it at that.

Vegan diets includes:

- *Strict no animal consumption*

- *Vegetables*

- *Fruits*

- *Whole Grains*

- *Nuts*

- *Seeds*

- *Berries*

- *Beans*

- *Soy or Tofu*

Mediterranean Diet

This diet has a rich history and cultural specificity, offering a lively timeline and time tested diet where the success is seen throughout all the cultures in the Mediterranean region. The positive and celebratory nature of the dining experience in these cultures is known throughout the world. This is why many travel to these regions simply to feast and enjoy life. This adheres to the theme throughout this book to build a relationship with food and eating that is positive and enjoyable. The people in the Mediterranean region are walking examples of the benefits of an enjoyable diet and food experience.

A Mediterranean shopping list may look similar to this:

- *Fruits*

- *Legumes*

- *Vegetables*

- *Fresh Fish*

- *Olive Oil*

The lean, low calorie and high-fat content of this diet make for a balanced diet that syncs well with an intermittent fasting routine. The relationship we build with our bodies should be enjoyable and shameless, pick a night to prepare a Mediterranean feast accompanied by a red wine from the region to break away from your usual routine.

Ketogenic Diet

We need to reiterate the dangers involved with inducing an intentional state of ketosis. If you are considering this type of diet, be sure to do your research and listen to your body. Let's discuss the ketogenic diet in more detail. Diets that adhere to a ketogenic structure are not typically practiced by beginners in the intermittent fasting communities. The diet is considered to be a more advanced structure than other popular diets. These diets are typically high in fat and very low in carbohydrate content. Whole grains and bread are avoided.

Some mandatory **foods** would be:

- *Eggs*

- *Avocados*

- *Fatty meats*

- *Fish*

The reasoning for this diet comes from the science of ketosis we touched on earlier in the book. By limiting caloric intake and lessening the quick energy we get from sugars and carbs, our bodies will burn stored fat cells as an alternative. Fat cells are cleaner and more efficient energy as well; this is why we see plenty of fats in a ketogenic diet. We can see here how ketogenic states are induced through a type of intermittent fast. Essentially, you fast from caloric intake and reach a state of ketosis. This is a very distinct reaction that the body is equipped with, acting as a survival instinct of the most evolved form.

Cutting back carbohydrates may seem simple but we need to realize that bread is off limits, as well as other starchy foods like rice and potatoes. A standard for ketogenic structured diets s to cut back carbohydrate consumption to 50-60 grams per day or less. Keep this up for five or six days and the body will begin to produce ketones. Now the body is forced to use stored fat for energy. This is literally shedding your excess fat. This state should not be kept up for too long or a detrimental effect can occur. Ketoacidosis can be very dangerous as the blood becomes too acidic. This is not a desired result of ketogenic diets. Be wise when practicing this diet and always listen to your body.

So the Ketogenic diet is probably the most effective to achieve healthy weight loss but should be reserved for those who have experience with intermittent fasting and other dieting experiences.

Chapter 11: Recipes

Breakfast

Zucchini Omelette

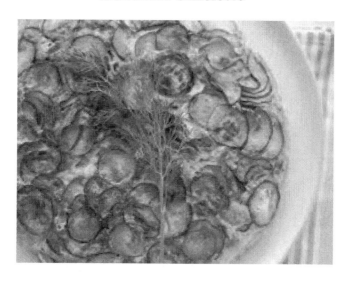

Servings: 6

Preparation time: 4 minutes

Cooking time: 3 hours and 30 minutes

Ingredients:

- 1½ cups red onion, chopped
- 1 tablespoon olive oil
- 2 garlic cloves, minced

- 2 teaspoons fresh basil, chopped
- 6 eggs, whisked
- A pinch of sea salt and black pepper
- 8 cups zucchini, sliced
- 6 ounces fresh tomatoes, peeled, crushed

Instructions:

1. In a bowl, mix all the ingredients except the oil and the basil.
2. Grease the slow cooker with the oil, spread the omelette mix in the bowl, cover and cook on low for 3 hours and 30 minutes.
3. Divide the omelette between plates, sprinkle the basil on top and serve for breakfast.

Chili Omelette

Servings: 4

Preparation time: 5 minutes

Cooking time: 3 hours and 30 minutes

Ingredients:

- 2 garlic cloves, minced
- 1 tablespoon olive oil
- 1 red bell pepper, chopped
- 1 small yellow onion, chopped
- 1 teaspoon chili powder
- 2 tablespoons tomato puree
- ½ teaspoon sweet paprika

- A pinch of salt and black pepper
- 1 tablespoon parsley, chopped
- 4 eggs, whisked

Instructions:

1. In a bowl, mix all the ingredients except the oil and the parsley and whisk them well.
2. Grease the slow cooker with the oil, add the egg mixture, cover and cook on low for 3 hours and 30 minutes.
3. Divide the omelette between plates, sprinkle the parsley on top and serve for breakfast.

Basil and Cherry Tomato Breakfast

Servings: 4

Cooking time: 4 hours

Preparation time: 4 minutes

Ingredients:

- 1 tablespoon olive oil
- 2 yellow onions, chopped
- 2 pounds cherry tomatoes, halved
- 3 tablespoons tomato puree
- 2 garlic cloves, minced
- A pinch of sea salt and black pepper
- 1 bunch basil, chopped

Instructions:

1. Grease the slow cooker with the oil, add all the ingredients, cover and cook on high for 4 hours.
2. Stir the mixture, divide it into bowls and serve for breakfast.

Carrot Breakfast Salad

Servings: 4

Preparation time: 5 minutes

Cooking time: 4 hours

Ingredients:

- 2 tablespoons olive oil
- 2 pounds baby carrots, peeled and halved

- 3 garlic cloves, minced
- 2 yellow onions, chopped
- ½ cup vegetable stock
- 1/3 cup tomatoes, crushed
- A pinch of salt and black pepper

Instructions:

1. In your slow cooker, combine all the ingredients, cover and cook on high for 4 hours.
2. Divide into bowls and serve for breakfast.

Garlic Zucchini Mix

Servings: 6

Preparation time: 5 minutes

Cooking time: 6 hours

Ingredients:

- 4 cups zucchinis, sliced
- 2 tablespoons olive oil
- 1 teaspoon Italian seasoning
- A pinch of salt and black pepper
- 1 teaspoon garlic powder

Instructions:

1. In your slow cooker, mix all the ingredients, cover and cook on Low for 6 hours.
2. Divide into bowls and serve for breakfast.

Crustless Broccoli Sun-dried Tomato Quiche

Servings: 6

Preparation time: 4 minutes

Cooking time: 3 hours and 30 minutes

Ingredients:

- 12.3-ounce box extra-firm tofu drained and dried
- 1 ½ cup broccoli, chopped
- 2 leeks, cleaned and sliced; both white and green parts
- 2 tablespoons vegetable broth
- 3 tablespoons nutritional yeast
- 2 chopped cloves of garlic

111

- 1 lemon, juiced
- 2 teaspoons yellow mustard
- 1 tablespoon tahini
- 1 tablespoon cornstarch
- ¼ cup old fashioned oats
- ½ teaspoon turmeric
- 3-4 dashes Tabasco sauce
- ½-1 teaspoon salt
- ½ cup artichoke hearts, chopped
- 2/3 cup tomatoes, sun-dried, soaked in hot water
- 1/8 cup vegetable broth

Instructions:

1. Preheat your oven to 375° F.
2. Prepare a 9" pie plate or springform pan with parchment paper or cooking spray.
3. Put all of the leeks and broccoli on a cookie sheet and drizzle with vegetable broth, salt, and pepper. Bake for about 20-30 min.
4. In the meantime, add the tofu, garlic, nutritional yeast, lemon juice, mustard, tahini, cornstarch, oats, turmeric, salt, and a few dashes of Tabasco in a food processor. When the mixture is smooth, taste for heat and add more Tabasco as needed.
5. Place cooked vegetables with artichoke hearts and tomatoes in a large bowl. With a spatula, scrape in tofu mixture from the processor. Mix carefully, so all of the vegetables are well

distributed. If the mixture seems too dry, add a little vegetable broth or water.

6. Add mixture to pie plate muffin tins, or springform pan and spread evenly.

7. Bake for about 35 min. or until lightly browned.

8. Cool before serving. It is delicious, both warm and chilled!

Chocolate Pancakes

Servings: 6

Preparation time: 5 minutes

Cooking time: 80 minutes

Ingredients:

- 1 ¼ cup gluten-free flour of choice
- 1 tablespoon ground flaxseed
- 1 tablespoon baking powder
- 3 tablespoons nutritional yeast
- 2 tablespoons unsweetened cocoa powder
- ¼ teaspoon of sea salt
- 1 cup unsweetened, unflavored almond milk
- 1 tablespoon vegan mini chocolate chips (optional)
- 1 teaspoon vanilla extract
- ¼ teaspoon stevia powder or 1 tablespoon pure maple syrup
- 1 tablespoon apple cider vinegar
- ¼ cup unsweetened applesauce.

Instructions:

1. Get a medium bowl and mix all the dry ingredients (flour, baking powder, flaxseed, cocoa powder, yeast, salt, and optional chocolate chips). Whisk until evenly combined.

2. In a separate small bowl, combine wet ingredients except for the applesauce (almond milk, vanilla extract, apple cider vinegar, maple syrup, or stevia powder).

3. Add wet ingredient mixture and applesauce to the dry ingredients and mix by hand until ingredients are just combined.

4. The batter should sit for 10 minutes. It will rise and thicken, possibly doubling in size.

5. Heat an electric griddle or nonstick skillet to medium heat and spray with a small amount of nonstick spray, if desired. Scoop batter into 3-inch rounds. Much like traditional pancakes, bubbles will start to appear. When bubbles start to burst, flip pancakes and cook for 1-2 minutes. Yields 12 pancakes.

Breakfast Scramble

Servings: 7

Preparation time: 5 minutes

Cooking time: 60 minutes

Ingredients:

- 1 large head cauliflower, cut up
- 1 seeded, diced green bell pepper
- 1 seeded, diced red bell pepper
- 2 cups sliced mushrooms (approximately 8 oz whole mushrooms)
- 1 peeled, diced red onion
- 3 peeled, minced cloves of garlic
- Sea salt
- 1 ½ teaspoons turmeric
- 1–2 tablespoons of low-sodium soy sauce
- ¼ cup nutritional yeast (optional)
- ½ teaspoon black pepper

Instructions:

1. Sauté green and red peppers, mushrooms, and onion in a medium saucepan or skillet over medium-high heat until onion is translucent (should be 7–8 min). Add an occasional tablespoon or two of water to the pan to prevent vegetables from sticking.

2. Add cauliflower and cook until florets are tenders. It should be 5 to 6 minutes.

3. Add, pepper, garlic, soy sauce, turmeric, and yeast (if using) to the pan and cook for about 5 minutes.

Lunch

Vegan Tuna Salad

Servings: 6

Preparation time: 5 minutes

Cooking time: 55 minutes

Ingredients:

- 2 cans chickpeas
- 1 tablespoon prepared yellow mustard
- 2 tablespoons vegan mayonnaise
- 1 tablespoon jarred capers
- 2 tablespoons pickle relish
- ½ cup chopped celery

Instructions:

1. In a medium bowl, combine chickpeas, mustard, vegan mayo, and mustard. Pulse in a food processor or mash with a potato masher until the mixture is partially smooth with some chunks.

2. Add the remaining ingredients to the chickpea mixture and mix until combined.

3. Serve immediately or refrigerate until ready to serve.

Veggie Wrap with Apples and Spicy Hummus

Servings: 6

Preparation time: 5 minutes

Cooking time: 40 minutes

Ingredients:

- 1 tortilla of your choice: flour, corn, gluten-free, etc.
- 3-4 tablespoons of your favorite spicy hummus (a plain hummus mixed with salsa is good, too!)
- A few leaves of your favorite leafy greens
- ¼ apple sliced thin
- ½ cup broccoli slaw (store-bought or homemade are both good)
- ½ teaspoon lemon juice
- 2 teaspoons dairy-free, plain, unsweetened yogurt
- Salt and pepper to taste

Instructions:

1. Mix broccoli slaw with lemon juice and yogurt. Add pepper and salt to taste and mix well.

2. Lay tortilla flat.

3. Spread hummus all over the tortilla.

4. Lay down leafy greens on hummus.

5. On one half, pile broccoli slaw over lettuce. Place apples on top of the slaw.

6. Starting with the half with slaw and apples, roll tortilla tightly.

7. Cut in half if desired and enjoy!

Turmeric Rack of Lamb

Servings: 4

Preparation time: 15 minutes

Cooking time: 16 minutes

Ingredients:

- 13 oz rack of lamb

- 1 tablespoon ground turmeric

120

- ½ teaspoon chili flakes
- 3 tablespoons olive oil
- 1 tablespoon balsamic vinegar
- 1 teaspoon salt
- ½ teaspoon peppercorns
- ¾ cup of water

Instructions:

1. In the shallow bowl, mix up together ground turmeric, chili flakes, olive oil, balsamic vinegar, salt, and peppercorns.
2. Brush the rack of lamb with the oily mixture generously.
3. After this, preheat grill to 380° F.
4. Place the rack of lamb in the grill and cook it for 8 minutes from each side.
5. The cooked rack of lamb should have a light crunchy crust.

Sausage Casserole

Servings: 6

Preparation time: 10 minutes

Cooking time: 35 minutes

Ingredients:

- 2 jalapeno peppers, sliced
- 5 oz Cheddar cheese, shredded
- 9 oz sausages, chopped
- 1 tablespoon olive oil
- ½ cup spinach, chopped
- ½ cup heavy cream
- ½ teaspoon salt

Instructions:

1. Brush the casserole mold with the olive oil from inside.
2. Then put the chopped sausages in the casserole mold in one layer.
3. Add chopped spinach and sprinkle it with salt.
4. After this, add sliced jalapeno pepper.
5. Then make the layer of shredded Cheddar cheese.
6. Pour the heavy cream over the cheese.
7. Preheat the oven to 355° F.
8. Transfer the casserole in the oven and cook it for 35 minutes.
9. Use the kitchen torch to make the crunchy cheese crust of the casserole.

Cajun Pork Sliders

Servings: 4

Preparation time: 10 minutes

Cooking time: 45 minutes

Ingredients:

- 4 low carb bread slices
- 14 oz pork loin
- 2 tablespoons Cajun spices
- 1 tablespoon olive oil
- 1/3 cup water

- 1 teaspoon tomato sauce

Instructions:

1. Rub the pork loin with Cajun spices and place in the skillet.
2. Add olive oil and roast it over the high heat for 5 minutes from each side.
3. After this, transfer the meat in the saucepan, add tomato sauce and water.
4. Stir gently and close the lid.
5. Simmer the meat for 35 minutes.
6. Slice the cooked pork loin.
7. Place the pork sliders over the bread slices and transfer in the serving plates.

Mac and Cheese Bites

Servings: 5

Preparation time: 5 minutes

Cooking time: 50 minutes

Ingredients:

- 1 ½ cups uncooked macaroni (gluten-free will work if needed)
- 1 medium onion, chopped (can substitute with 1 medium yellow pepper if you don't care for onions.)
- 1 clove garlic, chopped
- 2 tablespoons cornstarch, or arrowroot powder
- 1 cup non-dairy milk

- ½ teaspoon smoked paprika (can substitute for chipotle powder)
- 1 teaspoon lemon juice or apple cider vinegar
- ½ cup nutritional yeast
- 1 teaspoon salt

Instructions:

1. Preheat your oven to 350° F.

2. Prepare the muffin tin with liners.

3. Prepare macaroni according to instructions.

4. While macaroni is cooking, sauté garlic and onion (or substitute of choice) until it is just starting to turn golden brown. This can be done in a dry pan, but adding some oil will work as well.

5. Add garlic, onion, and all other non-macaroni ingredients into a blender and mix until smooth.

6. Drain the macaroni and return to the pan.

7. Pour sauce over macaroni and stir well.

8. Spoon mixture into muffin tin, stirring occasionally in between such an equal amount of sauce goes in each cup.

9. Push down tops with the back of a spoon.

10. Bake in the oven for 30 min.

11. Serve once cooled.

Chicken Salad with Cranberries and Pistachios

Servings: 6

Preparation time: 5 minutes

Cooking time: 80 minutes

Ingredients:

- 1 ½ cups dry soy curls (textured vegetable protein)
- 2 dashes apple cider vinegar
- ½ cup diced granny smith apples (approx. 1 small apple)
- ¼ cup shelled pistachios, chopped
- ½ cup dried cranberries
- 5-6 tablespoons veganaise (adjust depending on how creamy you would like the salad to be)
- 1 teaspoon of sea salt

- A pinch of thyme

Instructions:

1. Soak soy curls in warm water for 10 min. Squeeze excess water out of them and roughly chop larger pieces. Set aside.

2. While soy curls are soaking, mix diced apple and vinegar. Drain any excess liquid.

3. Combine apples with all other ingredients in large bowl until ingredients are evenly mixed. Add seasoning to taste. Chill for at least 30 minutes. Serve as desired.

Dinner

Pan-fried Jackfruit over Pasta with Lemon Coconut Cream Sauce

Servings: 6

Preparation time: 5 minutes

Cooking time: 30 minutes

Ingredients:

- 1 lb. pasta of choice
- 2 cans jackfruit in brine
- 2 tablespoons flour of choice
- Garlic powder, dried oregano, paprika, black pepper, kosher salt to taste

- 2 tablespoons vegetable oil
- 4 tablespoons vegan butter
- 2 cups of coconut milk
- Juice of 1 lemon
- 2 tablespoons grated vegan parmesan cheese
- 1 pinch ground nutmeg
- 1 teaspoon lemon zest (can use the same lemon from juice)
- Fresh basil leaves, chopped for garnish

Instructions:

1. Cook pasta until al dente. Drain the pasta but reserve 1 cup of the pasta water. Set it aside for now.

2. While the pasta is cooking, drain the jackfruit and cut each piece in half. Pat jackfruit dry.

3. Mix flour with garlic powder, oregano, paprika, pepper, and salt in a separate bowl.

4. Toss flour mixture with jackfruit.

5. Heat vegetable oil in a skillet. Pan-fry the jackfruit until crisp on both sides. It takes around ten minutes in total.

6. Transfer the jackfruit to a plate lined with a paper towel and set aside.

7. In a large saucepan or skillet, melt vegan butter. Add coconut milk and lemon juice. Then add parmesan cheese and nutmeg. Cook until sauce is thick.

8. Add cooked pasta and half of the reserved pasta water to skillet. Toss to coat all pasta.

9. Cook until everything is hot and the sauce is to desired consistency and pasta is heated through. If the sauce is too thick, continue to use remaining pasta water.

10. Turn off heat. Add lemon zest and add pepper and salt to taste. Sprinkle parmesan and basil leaves. Add pan-fried jackfruit on top when serving.

Butternut Squash Tacos with Tempeh Chorizo

Servings: 5

Preparation time: 5 minutes

Cooking time: 50 minutes

Ingredients:

- One 8-ounce package tempeh
- ½ cup of filtered water
- ¼ cup apple cider vinegar
- 2 cups butternut squash, peeled, cut into cubes
- 1 teaspoon chili powder
- ½ teaspoon smoked paprika
- ½ teaspoon cumin
- ½ teaspoon garlic powder
- ½ teaspoon oregano
- A dash of cayenne
- 1 tablespoon nutritional yeast
- A few dashes of liquid smoke
- Black pepper and sea salt to taste
- ½ cup thinly julienned carrot (optional)
- 8 corn tortillas (or whatever you have on hand)
- 1 large avocado, pitted and sliced
- Cilantro, chopped

Instructions:

1. Cut the tempeh into two parts. Steam for 10 min. Place in a large bowl and tear apart into small pieces either with your hands (after it's cooled) or with a pastry cutter.

2. While tempeh is steaming, bring water and vinegar to a boil in a small skillet.

3. Add spices, squash, liquid smoke, nutritional yeast, and a pinch of sea salt to skillet. Coat well and simmer covered, stirring occasionally. Add carrots and tempeh, covering again. Simmer a little while longer, stirring to prevent sticking. Uncover and season with pepper and salt.

4. Fill warmed tortillas with squash and tempeh mix and top with avocado and cilantro.

Coated Cauliflower Head

Servings: 6

Preparation time: 10 minutes

Cooking time: 40 minutes

Ingredients:

- 2-pound cauliflower head
- 3 tablespoons olive oil
- 1 tablespoon butter, softened
- 1 teaspoon ground coriander

- 1 teaspoon salt
- 1 egg, whisked
- 1 teaspoon dried cilantro
- 1 teaspoon dried oregano
- 1 teaspoon tahini paste

Instructions:

1. Trim cauliflower head if needed.
2. Preheat oven to 350° F.
3. In the mixing bowl, mix up together olive oil, softened butter, ground coriander, salt, whisked egg, dried cilantro, dried oregano, and tahini paste.
4. Then brush the cauliflower head with this mixture generously and transfer in the tray.
5. Bake the cauliflower head for 40 minutes.
6. Brush it with the remaining oil mixture every 10 minutes.

Artichoke Petals Bites

Servings: 8

Preparation time: 10 minutes

Cooking time: 10 minutes

Ingredients:

- 8 oz artichoke petals, boiled, drained, without salt
- ½ cup almond flour
- 4 oz Parmesan, grated
- 2 tablespoons almond butter, melted

Instructions:

1. In the mixing bowl, mix up together almond flour and grated Parmesan.
2. Preheat the oven to 355° F.

3. Dip the artichoke petals in the almond butter and then coat in the almond flour mixture.
4. Place them in the tray.
5. Transfer the tray in the preheated oven and cook the petals for 10 minutes.
6. Chill the cooked petal bites little before serving.

Stuffed Beef Loin in Sticky Sauce

Servings: 4

Preparation time: 15 minutes

Cooking time: 6 minutes

Ingredients:

- 1 tablespoon Erythritol
- 1 tablespoon lemon juice
- 4 tablespoons water
- 1 tablespoon butter

- ½ teaspoon tomato sauce
- ¼ teaspoon dried rosemary
- 9 oz beef loin
- 3 oz celery root, grated
- 3 oz bacon, sliced
- 1 tablespoon walnuts, chopped
- ¾ teaspoon garlic, diced
- 2 teaspoons butter
- 1 tablespoon olive oil
- 1 teaspoon salt
- ½ cup of water

Instructions:

1. Cut the beef loin into the layer and spread it with the dried rosemary, butter, and salt.
2. Then place over the beef loin: grated celery root, sliced bacon, walnuts, and diced garlic.
3. Roll the beef loin and brush it with olive oil.
4. Secure the meat with the help of the toothpicks.
5. Place it in the tray and add a ½ cup of water.
6. Cook the meat in the preheated to 365° F oven for 40 minutes.
7. Meanwhile, make the sticky sauce: mix up together Erythritol, lemon juice, 4 tablespoons of water, and butter.
8. Preheat the mixture until it starts to boil.
9. Then add tomato sauce and whisk it well.

10. Bring the sauce to boil and remove from the heat.

11. When the beef loin is cooked, remove it from the oven and brush with the cooked sticky sauce very generously.

12. Slice the beef roll and sprinkle with the remaining sauce.

Vegan Fish Sticks and Tartar Sauce

Servings: 6

Preparation time: 5 minutes

Cooking time: 80 minutes

Ingredients:

- *Fish Sticks:*

- 12-ounce package extra-firm tofu
- ½ cup cornmeal
- 1 tablespoon garlic powder
- 1 tablespoon dried basil
- 2 tablespoons dulse flakes
- 1 tablespoon onion powder
- ½ cup whole wheat flour (rice flour is a good gluten-free option)
- 10 turns fresh black pepper
- 1 tablespoon of sea salt
- ¼ cup non-dairy milk, unsweetened
- 1 cup high-heat oil for frying

- *Vegan Tartar Sauce:*
- ¼ cup sweet pickle relish
- ½ cup vegan mayo
- ½ teaspoon sugar
- ½ teaspoon lemon juice
- 5 turns fresh black pepper

Instructions:

1. Rinse tofu and drain in a colander. Placing a heavy plate on tofu with a heavy item on top will help drain better. Set it aside.

2. In a medium bowl, mix the flour, cornmeal, garlic powder, basil, onion powder, dulse flakes, pepper, and salt. Whisk together. Set the mix aside.

3. Set tofu on cutting board. Cut into quarters.

4. Slice tofu into thin pieces. You should have 28-32 pieces in total.

5. In a large cast-iron skillet, heat oil on medium/low heat.

6. In a small bowl, pour non-dairy milk.

7. Dip each piece of tofu in non-dairy milk. Immediately dip in breading, coating all sides evenly. Repeat until all pieces are coated.

8. The oil will start to splatter when hot enough. At that point, add tofu pieces to skillet. Repeat until all pieces are cooked.

9. Each side will cook for about 2-3 minutes. Watch for golden brown color. Place tofu pieces on a brown paper bag as you remove them from pan to soak up excess oil.

10. Repeat as necessary until all tofu is cooked. Cool before serving. Mix all tartar sauce ingredients until an even and creamy sauce is made. Enjoy!

Vegan Philly Cheesesteak

Servings: 4

Preparation time: 5 minutes

Cooking time: 40 minutes

Ingredients:

- 6-8 sliced Portobello mushrooms
- 4 cloves garlic, minced

- 1 tablespoon olive oil
- 1 whole clove garlic
- ½ teaspoon black pepper
- 1 teaspoon dried thyme
- ½ large diced onion
- A dash of kosher salt
- 1 tablespoon vegan Worcestershire sauce
- Hoagie rolls or another small loaf of bread of choice
- 1 cup shredded vegan cheddar cheese
- Vegan mayo (optional)

Instructions:

1. Preheat the broiler.

2. In a deep skillet, heat olive oil. Brown mushrooms in oil, about 10 min.

3. Add thyme, garlic, and pepper until evenly coated.

4. Add onion and salt. Mushrooms must be well cooked before adding salt. Cook until onion is caramelized and softened, which should be for about 5 minutes. Add Worcestershire sauce and mix well.

5. Slice the bread lengthwise. Coat open sides of bread with olive oil or cooking spray. To add garlic flavor, cut the whole garlic clove, cut off the tip, and put on the oiled side of bread. Garlic powder is also a good substitute.

6. If desired, add optional vegan mayo. Place bread on cookie sheet. Fill loaves with mushrooms and top with shredded vegan cheddar cheese.

7. Place in broiler until cheese has melted, which should be 4-5 minutes.

Desserts

Mango Lime Chia Pudding

Servings: 3

Preparation time: 5 minutes

Cooking time: 30 minutes

Ingredients:

- 3 cups fresh or frozen mango chunks
- One 15.5-ounce can coconut milk
- 1 tablespoon lime zest

- ¼ cup maple syrup

- ¼ cup freshly squeezed lime juice

- ¼ cup hemp seeds

- 1/3 cup chia seeds

- *Topping options:* Approximately 8 cups of any combination of mango, banana, pineapple, or any fruit you'd love with mango and lime. (Banana is a fruit you'd want to wait to add until you are ready to eat the pudding as it browns and gets mushy very quickly once out of its peel)

Instructions:

1. Place mango chunks, coconut milk, lime zest, and maple syrup in a blender. Mix until smooth.

2. Add hemp and chia seeds in the blender and stir by hand or blend on low to just combine.

3. This should yield 4 cups of pudding. Portion it as you prefer. One suggestion is to divide into 8 portions, one each in a pint jar, and top with one cup of fresh fruit.

4. Refrigerate pudding until ready to eat, minimum 4 hours to set. The pudding keeps for 5-7 days.

Mint Chocolate Truffle Larabar Bites

Servings: 6

Preparation time: 5 minutes

Cooking time: 45 minutes

Ingredients:

- 1 cup vegan chocolate chips (semi-sweet dark chips are recommended)
- 10 large Medjool dates
- 1 ½ cups of raw almonds
- ¼ cup coconut flour

- ¼ cup of cocoa powder
- ¼-1/2 teaspoon peppermint extract
- 2 tablespoons water

Instructions:

1. Pour almonds into a food processor and chop until a fine flour.

2. Add chocolate chips, dates, flour and cocoa, and process again until well combined.

3. Add oil and peppermint extract.

4. Process one more time until the mix starts balling up.

5. Taste a small bit and add more peppermint if you wish. Process again if you do.

6. Remove the blade from the processor and form the dough into balls. Choose whatever size you like, as they do not need to bake and will be good in any portion.

Keto Chocolate Mousse

Servings: 6

Preparation time: 5 minutes

Cooking time: 40 minutes

Ingredients:

- Cocoa powder – .33 cup
- Lakanto monk fruit sweetener – 2 tablespoons
- Heavy whipping cream – 1.5 cups

Instructions:

1. Place the heavy cream in a bowl and use a hand mixer or stand mixer to beat it on medium speed.

2. Once the cream begins to thicken, add the monk fruit sweetener and cocoa and continue to beat it until stiff peaks form.

3. Serve the mousse immediately or store it in the fridge for up to twenty-four hours before enjoying it. If desired, you can serve it with Lily's stevia-sweetened chocolate for chunks.

No-Bake Peanut Butter Pie

Servings: 6

Preparation time: 5 minutes

Cooking time: 60 minutes

Ingredients:

- Almond flour – 1 cup
- Butter softened – 2 tablespoons
- Vanilla - .5 teaspoon
- Lakanto monk fruit sweetener – 1.5 tablespoons
- Cocoa powder – 3 tablespoons
- Cream cheese softened – 16 ounces

- Heavy cream – .75 cup

- Vanilla – 2 teaspoons

- Swerve confectioner's sweetener - .66 cup

- Peanut butter or Sun Butter, unsweetened – .75 cup

Instructions:

1. Combine the almond flour, butter, .5 teaspoon of vanilla, Lakanto sweetener, and cocoa powder in a bowl with a fork until it forms a crumbly mixture. Press this mixture into a nine-inch pie plate and then allow it to chill in the fridge while you prepare the filling.

2. In a large bowl, beat together the cream cheese, peanut butter, confectioners Swerve, and remaining vanilla until light and creamy. Using a spatula scrape down the sides of the bowl before adding in the heavy cream.

3. Beat the filling some more until the heavy cream is incorporated and the mixture is once again light and creamy.

4. Pour the filling into the prepared crust and allow it to chill for two hours before serving. Slice and enjoy.

Strawberries with Ricotta Cream

Servings: 6

Preparation time: 5 minutes

Cooking time: 40 minutes

Ingredients:

- Ricotta, whole milk – 1.5 cups
- Heavy cream – 2 tablespoons
- Lemon zest – 1.5 teaspoons
- Swerve confectioner's sweetener – .25 cup
- Vanilla extract – 1 teaspoon
- Blackberries - .5 cup
- Raspberries - .5 cup

- Blueberries - .5 cup

Instructions:

1. In a large bowl, add all of the ingredients, except for the berries, and whip them together with a hand mixer until completely smooth.

2. Set out four parfait glasses and divide half of the berries between all of them. Top the berries with half of the ricotta mixture, the remaining half of the berries, and lastly, the second half of the ricotta mixture.

3. Serve the parfaits immediately or within the next 24 hours.

Easy Chocolate Pudding

Servings: 6

Preparation time: 5 minutes

Cooking time: 30 minutes

Ingredients:

- 1 ½ cups organic coconut cream from a can
- ½ cup raw cacao powder (sifted unsweetened cocoa powder works as well)
- 6 tablespoons pure maple syrup (may adjust to up to 8 tablespoons, depending on how sweet you like it)
- 2 teaspoons pure vanilla extract
- Fine-grain sea salt

Instructions:

1. In a small saucepan over low heat, whisk coconut cream, cacao, and maple syrup until smooth. A smaller whisk my make a smoother mixture. Continue to cook over low/medium for 2 minutes, or until the mixture just starts to come to a boil with small bubbles.

2. Remove from heat. Add salt and vanilla. Stir. Taste and add more maple if you'd like a sweeter pudding.

3. Pour into individual containers/bowls or keep in one larger bowl to set.

4. Cover and refrigerate until set, or overnight for a thick and creamy pudding. Make 4 servings.

Chapter 12: 7 Day Meal Plan

DAY	BREAKFAST	LUNCH	DINNER	DESSERT
1.	Zucchini Omelet	Vegan Tuna Salad	Pan-fried Jackfruit over Pasta with Lemon Coconut Cream Sauce	Mango Lime Chia Pudding
2.	Chili Omelet	Veggie Wrap with Apples and Spicy Hummus	Butternut Squash Tacos with Tempeh Chorizo	Mint Chocolate Truffle Larabar Bites
3.	Basil and Cherry Tomato Breakfast	Turmeric Rack of Lamb	Coated Cauliflower Head	Keto Chocolate Mousse
4.	Carrot Breakfast Salad	Sausage Casserole	Artichoke Petals Bites	No-Bake Peanut Butter Pie
5.	Garlic Zucchini Mix	Cajun Pork Sliders	Stuffed Beef Loin in Sticky Sauce	Berries with Ricotta Cream

6.	Crustless Broccoli Sun-dried Tomato Quiche	Mac and Cheese Bites	Vegan Fish Sticks and Tartar Sauce	Easy Chocolate Pudding
7.	Chocolate Pancakes	Chicken Salad with Cranberries and Pistachios	Vegan Philly Cheesesteak	Mango Lime Chia Pudding

Conclusion

Intermittent fasting is an amazing concept not only for losing weight but also for gaining holistic health benefits.

It is free of cost and easy to follow. This book was an attempt to explain the concept of intermittent fasting and the ways in which it can be incorporated in daily life for best results.

This book is especially for women as there are some differences in intermittent fasting methods for men and women. This book caters to the concept of intermittent fasting for women. It explains the reasons for the difficult weight loss journey experienced by women and the ways in which it can be made easier and productive.

If you've been postponing your fast, now is the best time to start. Getting healthy is a matter of life and death, quite literally. Do not let procrastination cost you your health, and possibly your life. Some of the people dealing with lifestyle diseases today wish they had taken such a move earlier.

Get an accountability partner to walk with you, or find a community of intermittent fasting enthusiasts. If you can't find them in your area, you can do so online. With a supportive company, you'll have an easier time getting into the fast and staying on course.

Keep your expectations realistic; especially on weight loss. Results vary from one individual to the other, so don't worry too much when you can't seem to lose as much weight as the others on the same plan. With persistence and disciple, you will begin to experience the positive changes pretty soon. Go on and enjoy your leaner body, improved body image, active lifestyle and a life free from the worries of disease.

The truth is: your healthy diet is not entirely about what you eat. It is also about when you eat! By eating in a way that follows your body's natural rhythms and needs, you maximize its ability to function healthily. This supports your body with everything from weight loss and muscle gain to balancing hormones and blood sugar levels. There are many different benefits that you stand to gain when you monitor not only what you eat, but when. Perhaps one of the best parts of intermittent fasting is that this unique diet does not require you to give up on anything that you truly enjoy eating. Instead, you simply change when you eat and enjoy less healthy food choices in moderation. Of course, if you prefer to combine intermittent fasting with another diet, such as the ketogenic diet, then you will have adjusted food requirements. However, the intermittent fasting diet itself does not require you to adjust your food intake to meet any specific needs.

It is also important that you take the time to regularly monitor your symptoms and pay attention to your needs. Listen to your body and what it is telling you, as this will support you in really embracing the diet in the most powerful way possible. You do not want to find yourself struggling to succeed because you have made it too challenging for yourself. Going slower and learning to truly listen to your needs now will make your long-term goals far more achievable and sustainable.

Thank you, and best of luck!

Printed in Great Britain
by Amazon